WE ARE SOLDIERS

OUR HEROES. THEIR STORIES.
REAL LIFE ON THE FRONT LINE.

DANNY DANZIGER

sphere

SPHERE

First published in Great Britain in 2010 by Sphere

Any individual contributions of a political nature are that of an
individual and not representative of the Secretary of State for Defence.

Maps drawn by John Gilkes.

A CIP catalogue record for this book
is available from the British Library.

ISBN HB 978-1-84744-396-0
ISBN CF 978-1-84744-397-7

Typeset in Garamond by M Rules
Printed and bound in Great Britain by
Clays Ltd, St Ives plc

Papers used by Sphere are natural, renewable and
recyclable products sourced from well-managed forests and certified
in accordance with the rules of the Forest Stewardship Council.

Mixed Sources
Product group from well-managed
forests and other controlled sources
www.fsc.org Cert no. SGS-COC-004081
© 1996 Forest Stewardship Council
FSC

Sphere
An imprint of
Little, Brown Book Group
100 Victoria Embankment
London EC4Y 0DY

An Hachette UK Company
www.hachette.co.uk

www.littlebrown.co.uk

Along the Paths, and through the Moors, Rob Jenkins
and Richard Oulton.
On the Camino, Rupert de Klee, Robert Devereux,
Eric Fairbairn, David Ogilvy – and Joe, of course –
Mungo Stormont and Robert Wilson-Wright.
For the Journey, my brother, James.

CONTENTS

COMBAT SERVICE SUPPORT

COMBAT SUPPORT ARMS

COMBAT ARMS

* denotes the use of a pseudonym, either at the request of the Ministry of Defence or the interviewees themselves.

THEATRES OF OPERATION

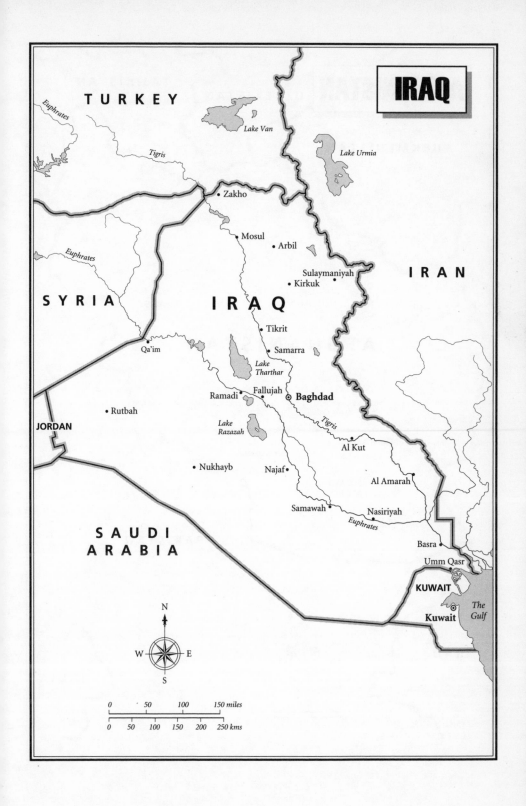

IRAQ

TURKEY

Euphrates

Tigris

Lake Van

Lake Urmia

• Zakho

• Mosul

• Arbil

Sulaymaniyah
• Kirkuk

IRAN

SYRIA

Euphrates

IRAQ

Qa'im

• Tikrit

• Samarra

Lake
Tharthar

• Rutbah

Ramadi
•

Fallujah
•

Tigris

⊙ Baghdad

Lake
Razazah

Al Kut
•

JORDAN

• Nukhayb

Najaf
•

Al Amarah •

Samawah •

Nasiriyah •

Euphrates

SAUDI
ARABIA

Basra •

Umm Qasr •

KUWAIT

The
Gulf

N

W   E

Kuwait ⊙

S

0   50   100   150 miles

0   50   100   150   200   250 kms

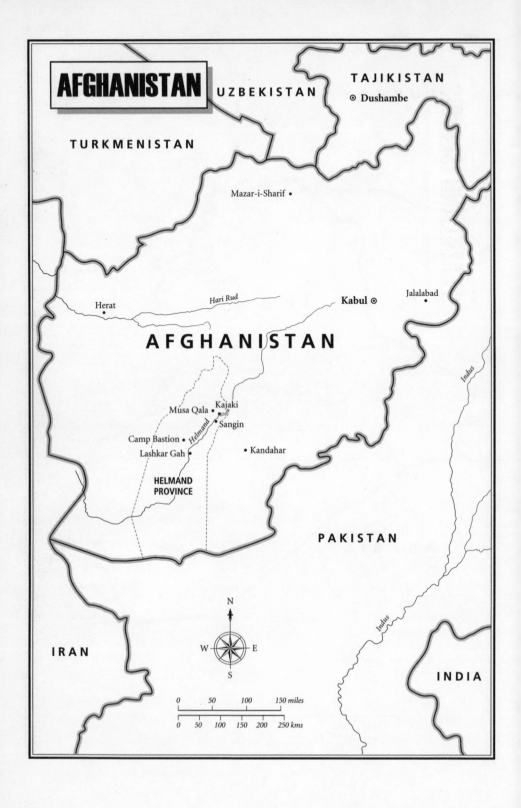

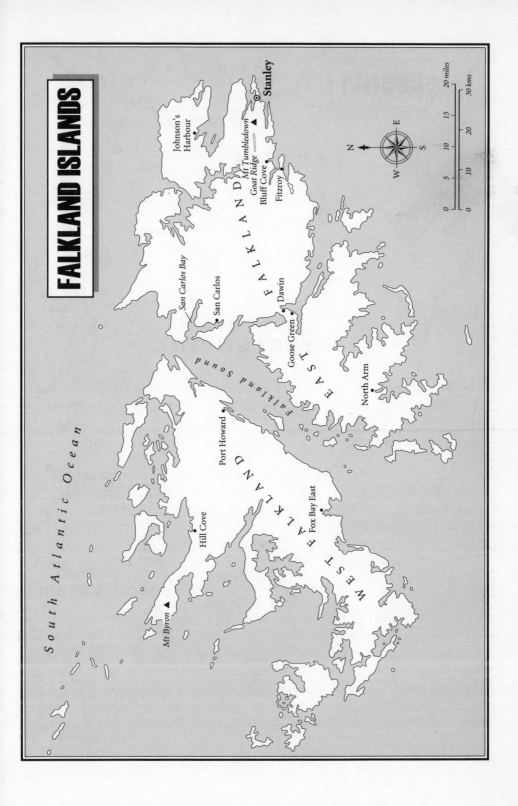

INTRODUCTION

I have had a taste of soldiering. It was a good many years ago and lasted approximately twelve hours, but it was incredibly exciting, slightly dangerous and physically taxing. I have never repeated it, nor have I forgotten it. In some ways I have always yearned to experience it again.

Late in the summer term of my final year at school, my headmaster – as a punishment for some now forgotten misdemeanour – tasked me to join a night exercise with the Officer Training Corps. Over the years he had disciplined me so many times and in so many ways that he had nearly run out of creative punishments. This was a new and original one.

Around 7 p.m. that evening, I joined the OTC boys on the bus, bound for an undisclosed bit of the English countryside, togged up in Army gear, which included complicated items like gaiters with buckles, webbing, heavy boots and an even heavier Lee-Enfield 303 rifle, loaned by a sceptical and reluctant quartermaster. My fellow travellers were the bigger lads in the school, fit and physically imposing. We had never really spoken to each other before; the atmosphere was one of unbridled testosterone.

We disembarked the bus in an area of almost unimaginable desolation, a terrain so challenging that I wondered whether we were still in the Home Counties. Divided into teams, we received maps and compo rations, and were told to meet up twelve hours later at a given location – thirty-five miles away. Even a logistical and geographical dunce like me knew that meant a long night and little sleep. And so it proved. As daylight turned into night, the balmy summer evening became cold and a piercing and unrelenting rain began to fall. We trudged on. At 3 a.m. we stopped for supper (or perhaps breakfast?). We cooked the rations – they consisted of baked beans and fragments of frankfurters in an indeterminate sauce – over fires we built ourselves. The tins, we later observed, had a bit of age to them – stamped on the sides was 'Ministry of Defence 1945'. Nevertheless, I have never since experienced a meal so delicious and satisfying.

The other lads were knowledgeable and clever with compasses and maps, and encouraged the straggler to keep up with their pace, rather than curse and berate me. Somehow I did keep up and we made it to the finishing point, and what is more, we arrived first.

At 10 a.m. exactly, an enormous helicopter, making a terrifying din, landed right among us and a general, with braids and medals (an old boy of the school), came down the steps to inspect the troops. As he walked up and down the lines, I could see out of the corner of my eye the major in charge of our OTC praying silently – the man's lips were moving – that the general would not come anywhere near me. But my bedraggled appearance and imperfect understanding of Army uniform – bits of my kit were coming undone – exercised some fascination for the general. He stopped in front of me and looked me over with an expression of horror, his face and bulging eyes an inch or two from mine. He pulled out his swagger stick from under his arm and flicked the back of my head with it. 'You, sir,' he barked, 'are the scruffiest example of a soldier I have ever seen.'

I don't know whether you can call the several subsequent days I spent nursing blistered feet part of that experience, but there were no more military adventures for me.

There are plenty of real adventures for the soldiers of the British Army today. For the past several years, like many others, I have followed their actions in Bosnia, in Iraq and in Afghanistan. I have watched the C-130 Hercules planes swooping into RAF Brize Norton with their cargo of fallen heroes. And I have wondered what kind of men they were and what it is like to be a soldier as wars rage around the world.

What do soldiers feel as they tend to wounded friends on the battlefield or engage in close combat, as an infantryman must be prepared to do? Or train their rifle sights on enemy soldiers and pull the trigger? What it is like to drive a Challenger tank over desert terrain for six days straight or parachute out of a Chinook helicopter?

I knew there was only one way to find out. Ask a soldier.

For the past year I have been travelling around the country, talking with serving soldiers of all ranks, from privates to generals. I think only by talking to them one-on-one can you get a real sense of what a soldier is truly like. They are different from other people. For instance, there is, I noticed, a characteristic that they all share: a calmness and purposeful intent. Nobody ever appears flustered or neurotic. 'If no one is going to die, then it doesn't matter' seems to be the attitude. There is an expression – maybe it's a philosophy – that I heard all the time in the Scottish regiments which sums it up perfectly: 'Nae drama.'

During my travels I spoke with Major Ian Lawrence about death on the battlefield, asked Padre Pat Aldred what the atmosphere was like before troops started an operation, and found out how injuries affect soldiers. By the end of the process I felt as though I had entered the jungles of Borneo with Colour Sergeant Wayne Harrod, a jungle survival expert; endured Arctic conditions alongside Lieutenant Colonel Andrew Jackson of 2 PARA; sat alongside Captain Tom Kelly as he negotiated with Afghan warlords; and witnessed the rescue of captured British soldiers in Sierra Leone with Sergeant Major Jimmy Fitzwater.

They are brave. Some of them are heroes. Got the citation and the medal. As someone who faces nothing more dangerous than a paper burn in his working life, I am interested by people who deliberately put themselves in dangerous situations, and the modesty with which they tell their stories.

It is these 'stories', these interviews, which I hope give the reader a real sense of what soldiering is like, both in the arena of war and in peace time. I hope also that they provide an understanding of the kind of people soldiers are. What makes men and women choose to be soldiers in the twenty-first century? Where do they find the desire to test themselves on the battlefield? Where does the intense loyalty to their regiments, and love for their fellow soldiers, come from? Some of the answers might surprise you. They did me. I didn't expect to hear about the enjoyment, satisfaction and sometimes sheer exuberance in doing such an exciting, dangerous job. This is a story of men and women performing their duties in difficult and challenging conditions – and loving every moment.

Danny Danziger

COMBAT SERVICE SUPPORT

The Combat Service Support provide sustainment and support for the Combat Arms and Combat Support Arms. While CSS personnel are not intended to engage the enemy, the fluidity of the modern battlefield means that these personnel are likely to be engaged in close combat at times, particularly when associated with battle groups.

Royal Logistic Corps

Corps of Royal Electrical and Mechanical Engineers

Royal Army Medical Corps

Royal Army Dental Corps

Queen Alexandra's Royal Army Nursing Corps

Royal Army Veterinary Corps

Adjutant General's Corps

Army Physical Training Corps

Corps of Army Music

Royal Army Chaplains' Department

Small Arms School Corps

PADRE PAT ALDRED

'Food and drink for the journey...'

I joined the Army as a chaplain with no Army experience what-soever. I didn't know a corporal from a colonel. When I donned my uniform, which is exactly the same Combat 95 uniform as the soldiers wear, I was not quite sure how to put it on. The only way anyone would know I'm a chaplain is that we wear combat crosses on our collars and don't carry weapons. We always need to have a soldier to look after us and act as a bodyguard and driver.

I started working with the King's Own Royal Border Regiment, a Cumbrian infantry regiment, and within three weeks found myself deployed on an operational tour in Macedonia, ready for the Kosovan conflict.

It was quite scary driving over the border, not knowing what we would find. Macedonia is a beautiful country, with snow-capped mountains and beautiful lakes. The country's president, Boris Trajkovski – who has since been assassinated – was a Methodist and a very prayerful man as well. He was incredibly brave in the vision he had for Macedonia and he tried to keep the country on track so that it would not disintegrate like Serbia and Bosnia. On the few occasions that we met up he was really excited to see me – he had never met a Methodist from England.

Out of all the welfare agencies, it is only the chaplain that actually deploys with soldiers. The duty of a chaplain is to be where the guys are and to loiter with intent. If they are going on patrol for the day, you can go out with them, so long as you are not getting in the way. Being away from home gives soldiers time to think, and they begin having to deal with things they may not have dealt with, or wanted to deal with, in years. That is a good opportunity to give them a listening ear, and I think the chaplain can be a real source of help to people then.

Soldiers get up to all sorts and will talk to you about absolutely anything. Lots of them may have seen and experienced dreadful things on the battlefield and want to offload to a chaplain. They worry about financial problems. They have affairs with people, so they may want to talk to you about marriage break-up, which is huge in the Army. Operations are a real make or break time for a family: the men are either going to come back stronger and renewed, and keep their marriage intact, or they are going to separate and divorce, and that will be the end of it.

Church is popular on operations. I always have full churches then, although to be on the safe side, I also tend to go around drumming up business, yelling at the top of my voice, 'Church is about to start.' Church can be anywhere. Sometimes we pull up in the middle of nowhere, drop the tailgate down and set up the Communion on the back of the wagon. A couple of times we pitched tents at one of Saddam's palaces in Basra. But wherever

4

we are, church is a place for soldiers to come away from the heat of battle, or whatever they are doing, and be reflective.

The service is always pretty simple, a couple of hymns and a short address, and, unlike most Methodists, every time we have worship I will give everyone the opportunity to take Communion. For some people there is something symbolic about bread and wine – food and drink for the journey, if you like. There is something sustaining in the act of taking Communion that draws people together and underlines that we are a team, one bread, one body.

I was on operational tour for Telic 1, when the Iraq war broke out. At that time I was in the Duke of Wellington's Regiment, an infantry regiment using Warrior armoured vehicles. We had not been destined to go to Iraq at all, but on a Friday afternoon the commanding officer called everyone on to the parade square and gave us the news that he was leaving for Iraq within the hour, and the rest of us would follow the next day, St Patrick's Day.

On the Kuwaiti border, the vehicles all lined up ready for the start, the engines were roaring, ammunition was being loaded into the guns, sergeant majors were yelling at the soldiers – I guess not a lot of that has changed since the First or Second World Wars. I remember going down the lines and columns of vehicles, wishing people all the best. A huge amount of people gave me personal stuff 'just in case' – a watch, a wedding ring or a necklace, and letters they had written to loved ones. In the end I had to keep an inventory. My words were, 'Don't worry it will be fine, I will give you this back tomorrow.'

It is a bit of a cliché, but that's the time I dish out a copy of

Psalm 23, which talks about going through the valley of the shadow of death and how the Lord is always with us. 'Just put it in your top pocket', I'll say. 'You never know when you might want to have a pray.'

As we were setting off, a missile landed in the camp. At that stage we all believed there were weapons of mass destruction ready to be used on us. I remember everybody reaching for respirators and donning NBC (nuclear, biological, chemical) suits, and running for cover into concrete bunkers situated around the camp. We now know there were no chemical weapons, but at the time we thought it was 'Operation Certain Death'. Yet there was real fighting and people were getting injured and killed. This was the real thing.

You see a certain amount of death in parish life through old age or illness, but when dealing with death in the Forces, it is always to the young and it is always tragic and cruel – life snatched away from people with whom you had been chatting and having a laugh that morning.

The first summer of Afghanistan will stay with me always. I was back in England, looking after the Royal Anglians and the Grenadier Guards. Everyone thought Afghanistan would be difficult, but nobody expected the toll to be so high – the Royal Anglians lost nine soldiers, which was quite a big shock for the whole regiment. Every week I found myself burying soldiers or being with parents who had just been told of the death of their son, or officiating at repatriation services at RAF Lyneham, where those killed in Afghanistan are brought. The military service, with military pallbearers and volleys of gunfire over the coffin, is very moving.

The death of a son is probably one of the hardest losses to bear. It is horrendous. Often, when the news is broken that their loved one has been killed, parents' first reaction is one of disbelief: 'It can't be true, I spoke with him last week.' Or, 'He's only eighteen . . .' People go into shock. But you can give no illusion at all. The notifying officers are given clear instruction so that the family are left in no doubt as to exactly what they have come to tell them. The officers don't use phrases like 'He's passed on' or 'He's been lost', just 'Your son has been killed, he's dead', as callous as that sounds.

I think one of the most difficult things for an Army chaplain is being with the recently bereaved. People look at you and say, 'Where's God in that now?' 'Why has this happened to me?' I don't have answers out of my top pocket particularly. I have lost my faith in lots of things. I have lost my faith in people quite often. Sometimes I lose my faith in the Church, but I haven't ever lost my faith in God.

Psalm 23 (King James version)

1. The LORD is my shepherd; I shall not want.

2. He maketh me to lie down in green pastures: he leadeth me beside the still waters.

3. He restoreth my soul: he leadeth me in the paths of righteousness for his name's sake.

4. Yea, though I walk through the valley of the shadow of death, I will fear no evil: for thou art with me; thy rod and thy staff they comfort me.

5. Thou preparest a table before me in the presence of mine enemies: thou anointest my head with oil; my cup runneth over.

6. Surely goodness and mercy shall follow me all the days of my life: and I will dwell in the house of the LORD for ever.

MAJOR STEPHEN BARNWELL

'Although my trade is musician, I am a soldier as well . . .'

As a kid I loved music. I was involved in youth orchestras and bands, and was very lucky to be born and bred in Nottingham, where instrumental lessons were free in school. Plus a person who had been a military musician taught me. His stories of the adventures he'd had were absolutely fascinating. They sounded so exciting. I wanted to sample some of that. At the age of sixteen, I left school with a bag of O levels and joined the Royal Artillery Band.

At that time the Artillery had a lot of regiments, which would have officers' mess dinners and the like. We would go and play 'for the benefit and well-being of the Royal Regiment of Artillery'. I have played wherever the Royal Artillery were mounting guard, and at Westminster Abbey. I have also played in St Paul's Cathedral for memorial services and state occasions. St Paul's is an awe-inspiring place to play, fantastic acoustics and quite flattering – the last note rings for five or six seconds and there is not a noise after that.

After completing three years of specialised training at the Royal Military School of Music at Kneller Hall, my very first appointment as a qualified bandmaster was at the Queen's Lancashire Regiment. Every twenty years the line regiments receive a new set of colours, and this particular year, the tercentenary of the regiment, coincided with the Presentation of Colours. Her Majesty the Queen was to present them. Oh, it was going to be a massive day. The battalion drilled and drilled with the band and the drums for weeks, and after a while we were immaculate.

However, come the day, the wind was howling a gale. It was literally force 7, plus it was teeming with rain and bitingly cold. But our commanding officer somehow managed to persuade the Queen that it would be a massive feather in her cap if she braved the elements rather than went in an aircraft hangar and did a watered down version of the parade. He must have had the gift of the gab because it was really ridiculous that she agreed.

The wind was so strong it was tearing the instruments away from the musicians' lips. Our bass drummer did an 180-degree turn after one particular gust got hold of his drum. He was facing exactly the wrong way, which was quite comical.

A few weeks later the regimental band went to do a royal garden party at Buckingham Palace – there is always a Household Division Guards' band at one end and a regimental or corps band at the other end by the lake. I was in the middle of conducting the band, when this rather smart-looking gentleman in a top hat and morning suit came over.

'Mr Barnwell?'

'Yes, it is,' I said.

'Her Majesty the Queen would like to speak with you.'

'What, now?'

'Yes, now.'

I handed the baton to my band sergeant major and went and stood in line. Her Majesty said hello – it turned out she wanted to know how she had done in the parade at Weeton. I told her, and it was the truth, that the people who attended the parade were incredibly impressed that she had braved the elements and continued in the face of adversity. I think she was pleased to hear that.

After I left the Band of the Queen's Lancashire Regiment, I was commissioned into the Corps of Army Music and became the deputy chief instructor at the Royal Military School of Music. Two further appointments as a director of music followed (Prince of Wales's Division (Clive) Band and the Irish Guards), before last November, at the age of fifty, I was reassigned to be musical director of the Welsh Guards Band for the final five years of my career. I was absolutely delighted because an appointment to one of the state bands, particularly the Foot Guards, is the pinnacle of a military musician's career.

The band of the Welsh Guards is among the top two state bands that perform at the moment. I won't even mention the name of the other band because that would be bigging them up and admitting it, wouldn't it? Besides, competition keeps things sharp. Well, I will admit some sections I've got are weaker than theirs, but then others are stronger. Do I have better woodwinds, which, for a military band, are incredibly important? Yes, I do, so therefore I would consider myself to have the premier band.

We have a wonderful balance of instruments. We have probably the best bassoonist in the Army and certainly the best oboist. Actually, everyone is very good. The band is established with nine clarinets, three flutes, two oboes (you usually only ever see one – there is a lack of oboists throughout the UK), four saxophones, four horns, eight trumpets, six trombones (although one's a bass), two bassoons (you're lucky if you have got one), two euphoniums, four tubas and three percussionists. And that little lot make an amazing sound.

The type of music you play for a concert is totally different from that you do on the parade ground. Indoors, you feel part of an ensemble, you can hear the music and feel everybody else around you, so it is easy to stay in tune and be sympathetic with the other instrumental sections that aren't as loud as you.

Playing outside, or 'on the hoof' as we call it, can give an edge and a harshness to the music. You have to get back into the practice room regularly to sand off those hard edges. You have to imagine what you sound like (as a band) because you can't hear properly, on account of the percussion section right across the middle: the wash of sound from the cymbals, bass drum and side drum, with a snare going, is a great big dividing line. The people at the front of the band don't have a clue what those at the back of the band are playing, because they can't hear each other. If they can't hear each other, are they in tune? You are rely- ing on the initial tuning note, but instruments warm up and the pitch changes slightly. So there are all sorts of problems playing outside. You have to be better than the average civilian musician and very confident as an individual.

We often have to play the national anthems of different countries, and we have to play them well. The Chinese national anthem is a nightmare for a conductor to remember and the

12

Argentinian one is pretty challenging too. But playing your own – well, it has got to be really special. You've got to raise your game. There is a danger you can pay lip service to something you do all the time, not do it justice, so we rehearse it frequently. Everyone knows the notes by heart of course, but it's a song and therefore it's about playing the correct phrase lengths. You have to be able to take enough air into your lungs to play complete phrases.

The British national anthem starts with a roll on the drums. It crescendos and then de-crescendos, and then we come in with the first beat, which is quite a low dynamic. The trumpet and trombone section don't play in the first half, giving it a *sotto voce* type of sound, and the second half of the anthem is *forte*. From the middle onwards it's slightly slower, *meno mosso*. It's marked. The whole anthem is in G, so it is the final chord of G major that comes via a falling dominant 7, which is usually the most audible part of the ending – and you know something's ended when it ends with a falling dominant 7, as if to say . . . that's it! It also ends with a *rallentando* of course, and a dotted minim that is held for as long as you dare – its length is in the heart of the conductor.

New music is the lifeblood of the band. If we don't change the repertoire, we will sound old and staid, and people will be bored. Recently I had to make a case for a budget for new music at a conference where they were talking about how much it cost to fire a tank round, and the cost of ammunition for live firing on the range. I said that new music to the band is like ammunition to the infantry – you can't fire spent ammunition, and old music would sound and feel like used ammunition.

We are really enjoying what we are playing at the moment. A particular contemporary overture called 'Full Tilt', by a chap called Richard Saucedo, is exciting for the audience to listen to and a challenge for the band to play, with strange chords and irregular time signatures. We always play a lot of Welsh tunes, good ones with martial airs, that lend themselves to being marched to, like 'Sospan Fach', 'We'll Keep a Welcome in the Hillsides', 'Men of Harlech', and 'God Bless the Prince of Wales'.

When the Welsh Guards go on guard at Buckingham Palace, it may seem we are playing to the hundreds of people behind the railings. But that is not actually my brief, according to the Household Division Standing Orders. I am really playing to keep the parade soldier's mind occupied when he is either being inspected or waiting for the guard change to complete. We will play modern things we think a twenty-year-old soldier wants to hear – anything from the latest film themes to something from the pop charts. At the moment we are playing 'You Can't Stop the Beat' from *Hairspray* – which was getting rowdy applause from the crowds the other day – and some things from *High School Musical 3* as well. We also do *Pirates of the Caribbean* and Harry Potter stuff, and classic songs like 'Simply the Best', 'Can You Feel the Love Tonight?' and tracks from *Grease*. We play a lot of music from the London shows because so many tourists go to them, and it is quite a treat to hear us play the songs. We also get out and about to play. We are permitted to do private commercial engagements for a fee. If you wanted to hire the Welsh Guards Band for an engagement, the all-in costs, with transport, VAT and our fees, would be about £7500.

In my thirty-four years in the Army, I have been operational only twice, which hitherto has been about the average for a musician. But I am glad that I had the experience because I'm always mindful that although my trade is musician, I am a soldier as well. I am proud to serve my Queen and country. I think I might have felt a little bit of an impostor if I had spent that long in the British Army and never seen any kind of action.

I went to Cookstown in Northern Ireland and Iraq, where I deployed with 34 Field Hospital in support of the Army Medical Services. It was the closest field hospital to the frontline there has ever been, within mortar range, and there were tank battles going on around us. The Royal Artillery was firing on Basra twenty-four hours a day. You could look out of the flaps of your tent at night and see the rounds going off like shooting stars through the sky. We did everything to support, from casualty tracking to guarding prisoners of war and digging latrines. We even buried amputated limbs in eight-figure grid references and logged them so that if they were dug up later, people would know the remains were from clinical work done by the hospital in the war.

There was a military band out there too and we played for church services. You would be surprised how many people go to church when they are about to go to war – virtually everybody on the camp will turn up to church parade. We keep to the standards, 'Abide With Me' and 'God Our Help in Ages Past'. Some keys are not good for communal singing and we usually play the hymns in a flat key so everyone can sing confidently.

Musicians are being asked to volunteer for battle right now. Individuals from the Welsh Guards Band have volunteered for Afghanistan and we have put those names forward. The Corps of Army Music needs five to go to Afghanistan each year and five to go off to other operations.

The Army has been a wonderful life for me. I may not be rich in monetary terms, but I feel rich to have done a job I would have willingly done for nothing in my spare time. The fact that I have been able to do it as my main employment, and paid to do it too, that's richness, that really is. So how lucky am I, really?

STAFF SERGEANT DAVID BRAHAM*

'There's no better piece of equipment than a dog . . .'

When I was doing my patrol dog handlers course, I got given a large German shepherd called Zak. He was a hard dog to handle because I'm quite a small-framed person. He was constantly pulling around and he was pretty unhelpful at squadded obedience too, because he didn't like other dogs. While you were trying to do your turns, nice and smart, all of a sudden he would move off to one side as he'd seen another dog. Like any animal, Zak understood how far he could push somebody, you know, 'Here's a new person, let's have a bit of fun with him.' Sometimes I would think, I'm never going to pass this course. But you learn more each day and all of a sudden the dog thinks, OK, he knows enough now, and everything falls into place.

You have two classifications of protection dogs and it all depends on what threat you've got as to which dog to use. One is what we call the patrol arm true, where the dog is trained to take only the right arm because most people hold a weapon in their right hand. The other type is the patrol dog, which has been made slightly more aggressive. He will bite anywhere on the body, and he can be used in various heightened situations.

Say you come across an intruder. You give the challenge nice and clear, so they fully understand what you mean: 'Halt, Army, or I will release my dog.' Then it is a step-by-step stage. You pull your dog closer into you, run your hands down his lead until you have hold of his collar, unclip his lead, and hold it away from his body, first so it won't get tangled in the dog's legs and also so you can say, 'Look, the dog's off his lead, I've only got hold of his collar, this is your last chance to stop ...' If the intruder stops and puts his hands up, you can clip your dog back on to the lead and close up the distance. If the intruder doesn't stop and is causing a threat to you or others, then it's your right at that time, according to the rules of engagement, to release the dog.

I deployed on my first operational tour with a protection dog to Lipjan Prison in Kosovo. On the top floor of this prison were Albanian prisoners who had committed war crimes and on the floor underneath were Serbian Croats, also guilty of war crimes.

My dog was a long-coated German shepherd by the name of Rory. His name matched what he did: he roared at anything that moved. If you've seen the cartoons of the Tasmanian Devil, when he's put in a box and suddenly the box starts shaking, well, that was Rory. But he was a focused and determined dog when it came to work, and very affectionate to the handler.

We used to allow about thirty prisoners into the exercise yard with one other person, namely me, making sure there was some form of control. As a handler, you often find themself the only person policing a location. With that one dog you can gain the situation and keep yourself safe at the same time. I never felt in any danger. I trusted Rory. He was a very good dog. No one wants to get bit by a dog, especially when they have seen what it can do. The prisoners could all see out of their cell windows and they had watched this dog attack a big padded suit in training.

When I left Kosovo, I handed Rory over to another handler, a friend of mine. He was very successful with Rory. In fact, he received a citation while he was out there, so it was a very good team.

It is awkward saying goodbye to your dog. If you have had that dog for a long time, there is a bond there. But you have to be able to break those bonds. Fortunately, you know he's going to another trainer, so the dog is going to be in good hands. He'll keep that person alive if he does his job correctly.

The next dog I had was called Sox, a Border collie, and, typical collie, very intelligent. I'd trained Sox as an arms explosive search dog and he and I did an operational deployment to the Army Dog Unit Northern Ireland, looking for IEDs (improvised explosive devices). Generally, gun dog breeds are used for that sort of work, so spaniels, Labradors, retrievers, collies and the odd Heinz-57. Three years I was with Sox and we had a very good relationship. Initially slightly aggressive, he would puff himself up and come towards you, growling. But he settled down and learned to trust me, and I learned to trust him. Eventually I could pick him up, throw him into a helicopter and off we would go around Northern Ireland.

My last search with Sox came in the Northern Ireland Canine Biathlon, an annual training competition event. He embarrassed me slightly because he decided he wasn't going to work. But he sort of knew I was leaving, so fair enough, no hard feelings. I still have pictures of him back home.

I was quite fearful that Sox might bite his new handler when I left, and I didn't want anything to happen to him because the implications of that can be quite severe for the dog – you can't have a person getting injured. Sox did have a little bit of an argument initially with his new trainer, but he settled down and went on to work with his new handler for the rest of his career.

For Iraq, where I was deployed twice, I picked up a German shorthaired pointer called Willow, a hunting dog who loves to run. You would let her off to search and she would cover an area so fast you'd wonder, 'Has she covered everything?' But we went out to Iraq twice and had quite a few finds, ranging from ammunition to explosive shells. You have to trust and rely on your dog, their hearing is a lot better than yours, their sense of smell is phenomenal compared to yours. Willow was very trustworthy. We came under fire once or twice but she was controlled and calm.

In military eyes, a dog is considered a piece of equipment. Well, there's no better piece of equipment, I'd say. A bulky X-ray machine can't manoeuvre around a battlefield as quickly as a dog and a handler, plus its batteries don't run out and it doesn't get a technical error because of a loose connection.

To the handler your dog is always going to be more than a piece of equipment. We are not mechanics, we can't put the spanner down on a Friday afternoon and come back Monday morning. We are there twenty-four/seven, 365 days a year. If we go on leave, someone else within our unit won't be going on leave because we have to look after those animals that are under our care. Because of that there's a huge bond. Dog handlers have the utmost respect for their animals: we are a team and the relationship between us is like no other.

Last year I volunteered to go to Afghanistan as I knew we were short of handlers there. Originally, I was going to get my dog in theatre, but the dog chosen had been in a few close bombardments and had stopped working effectively – dogs can get a form of shell shock, you know. So it wasn't until the actual day I flew to Afghanistan that I was given my search dog, Sasha, a yellow Labrador.

She turned out to be a brilliant dog and we had many successful finds. In fact, I had the most finds of anyone in my unit in the time I was on the ground. I handed Sasha over to another handler, Lance Corporal Ken Rowe, whose dog had stopped working effectively, while I assisted in running the unit. I hadn't known Ken long but we got on well. He was a bubbly young lad from Newcastle, very funny and easy to get along with, and we had quite a lot of banter between us.

A month later I heard the news that Ken had been killed in an ambush, along with Sasha. He was the first handler killed for many a year and that hit us quite hard because we are such a small unit, and are all close. It happened halfway through our tour. With three months to go, you've got to put it to one side, and do your grieving later, because you have to get on with the job. All the handlers came back in off the ground and attended Ken's repatriation in Camp Bastion. I was a coffin bearer in a six-man team and we carried him on to the plane, with the Unit Sergeant Major guiding us slowly and respectfully. Sasha was cremated, her ashes were put into an urn and she was placed on to the plane to one side of Ken – she wasn't carried beside Ken on the parade, because it was Ken's moment, but she was taken back to the UK with Ken and her ashes were offered to Ken's family

I have four dogs at home now. I have a retired tracker dog, who is a flat-coated retriever, and a Northern Inuit wolf cross malamute husky dog, who has different-coloured eyes, one brown, the other half-crested blue. I also have a brilliantly trained two-year-old German shepherd, my display model for when I go to dog training classes; and finally, I have a twelve-year-old German shepherd, who's tottering around now, she's so old. So there you are, four dogs at home. I'm not just a dog handler in the Army, but in every aspect of my life.

SERGEANT DANNY HARMER

'In front of my eyes . . .'

I am pretty much a self-taught photographer and I practised mostly using my dog, Beefy the Boxer, as a subject. One picture I took was such a nice portrait that everyone who saw it went, 'Hey, that's incredible.' Although whether that was luck or skill I don't know. I like to think it was a bit of both.

I enjoyed taking pictures and when I found out there was a trade of photographer in the Army, I decided to go for it. You can't join as a photographer, you have to transfer after you've got experience as a soldier. They want someone with military and tactical knowledge, who can take pictures without hindering soldiers or compromising their safety. But first of all, you have to face a panel of judges with a portfolio, and it is quite competitive because there are only about forty photographers in the whole of the Army.

So I upped my game, bought a digital SLR, read a bunch of books and eventually put together a portfolio of about twelve to fifteen images. I cringe when I look back at that portfolio now.

Certain ones were OK, but others were just point-and-click kind of shots – someone rock climbing, a sunset. But there must have been something the panel liked because I got the job. Maybe it was the portrait of old Beefy that I slipped in.

The kit we get issued from the Army is excellent, top-range Nikon D3Xs, the best Nikons you can get. They are about £5000 just for the body, and we receive two of those and three lenses – wide angle, mid-range and a long lens. We pretty much have the same kit as any photographer on a newspaper.

My first operation as an Army photographer was Telic 10 in Iraq. I did a seven-month tour as the brigade photographer for 1 Mechanised Brigade.

You definitely get the best pictures in action. Someone shooting a gun on the ranges back home may sound exactly the same as someone on operation in Iraq, but when it's for real the expressions on people's faces sell a picture: the panic, the stress and the excitement. The best pictures I took were of our guys storming a compound, going hell for leather, and pinning down rounds on an enemy position. I probably took about five hundred images that night.

Under the Geneva Convention, we are not allowed to show prisoners of war, and we have an unwritten rule that we don't film or photograph casualties. Just out of respect, if a soldier is dead, or life critical, I wouldn't even point my camera in that direction. But if a soldier is injured and going to be OK, we can photograph discreetly, without showing faces, or show medics treating the injured person.

No picture is worth dying for. If at any time I felt that my job as a photographer was putting someone else's or my own life on the line, then I would drop the cameras and use my weapon. At the end of the day, we are armed just like every other soldier.

Afghanistan was totally different from Iraq: more aggressive, more kinetic. You are constantly on edge, whether about where you're going to step next or about someone popping around the corner to shoot at you. I would challenge any soldier who says they are not scared or worried going out there. The terrain is a lot harder and the enemy you're fighting are better – they are always changing tactics to counter your tactics, and they are not afraid to stand up and fight, which you have to respect.

I was a photographer for Operation Panther's Claw. The first day, with people getting ambushed constantly and RPG'd, or stepping on IEDs, we only moved 1.5 kilometres forward. That's how slow it was. You would go three hundred metres or so and then get hit again. It started to get a bit depressing after you had been taking it all day and not given anything back.

Also, it is physically arduous. Compared with what the infantry soldiers have to carry, I can't complain, but as well as the two cameras, bits of camera kit and spare batteries in my bergen, I have got my rifle, Osprey armour that weighs nearly twenty kilos, magazines, spare rounds of ammunition, nine litres of water, rations and spare clothes. I am carrying around forty-five kilos in weight, and it is heavy and annoying. When nothing is happening, you kind of think, Oh, my shoulder and back really hurt. When stuff's happening, the last thing you worry about is the weight on your back.

You have to be tactically aware: if I switched off for a minute, that could be me gone. At times in Afghanistan I was half a metre away from stepping on an IED because I was looking for the photo and not at the ground. Rounds and RPGs, even though they're going to hurt if they hit, are stuff we consider fair, but it's the snideness of IEDs we don't like, the knowledge that you can't do anything about them.

Knowing the area so well, the Taliban ambush you where they can set IEDs so that you are always on the back foot. At one point, our front guy was searching for IEDs on a bridge and as he got a reading, the Taliban engaged us from a compound about two hundred metres in front. Basically, they wanted us to run into the IEDs planted around that area. Bubba, the platoon sergeant, shouted to us to follow him and he made a good call – or a lucky one. We stayed to the right of the bridge and instead of running down the track, ran across a crop field up to a tree line, and then about a hundred metres to a wall, where we started to engage the Taliban. As the guys went down into fire position and began firing, I started taking pictures, but when the enemy's rate of fire started to match ours, I chucked my cameras and engaged the Taliban. It was exhilarating and the firepower was soon too much for them. They stopped.

But they had hit one of the Scimitar tanks with an armour-piercing RPG, killing one of the guys in the back and seriously injuring another. We all had to stay where we were, secure the ground and call in the medical emergency response team (MERT). The Chinook came in and took the two guys. I got good pictures from a distance. As the Chinook took off, there was a massive explosion; someone had stepped on an IED. There were a lot of casualties and I saw things I don't think anyone should have to see. Even those soldiers that were ten metres away got thrown ten or fifteen metres. In one minute I had gone from being excited, full of adrenalin, actually shooting up Taliban and feeling like I was giving something back, to experiencing the worst feelings I have probably ever had.

At half-seven that evening, with the light fading, we had to give up the ground we had gained and go back about four hundred metres to a compound to set up for the night, to take on some food, get watered down and look forward to the next day.

Everyone was knackered. After battle you feel really tired. Every time I have gone out on patrol I've never slept so well – it has been some of the best kip I have had. You try and take off as many clothes as possible so they can dry, and put on some clean ones just for the night, and pretty much as soon as your head hits the pillow – yeah, I had brought a little travel pillow, got to have some comforts – you are out like a light.

At half-four, five o'clock, the next morning it was pretty much up straight away, helmet and body armour back on, sitting there waiting for something to happen. And same again the following day. After four days, I decided to get myself off the ground so I could send material out to the press. Me and Naz, the video guy, got moved back to the rear echelon, and took a vehicle and moved out to FOB Price, a secure camp that has power, where we could edit and upload with our portable satellites. I had already chosen the images I wanted to send out, so it was just a matter of transferring them to the computer, putting on the file information, resizing and sending them via the satellite. Soldiers, especially in operational theatres, are very happy if they see material being used in magazines and newspapers – and if you get a picture of one of them on the front page of the *Sun*, they're over the moon.

I got back from Afghanistan four days ago. My wife came and picked me up from Brize Norton. I purposely hadn't shaved for a couple of days to look a bit a more 'warry'. We had some champagne and dinner, and the first thing I did, after kissing and cuddling the wife, was to play with the dog, old Beefy, who's eight now and still plodding on.

I try not to dwell on it too much, but I am still a little bit sad about some of the things I've seen. I just hope that all our efforts have helped improve the situation out there.

MAJOR GENERAL ALAN HAWLEY
'A very bad prognosticator ...'

I had done some operational tours of Northern Ireland and seen things, the usual things going on at the time, riots and bombs. The first time I saw a shooting brought home to me how arbitrary and completely random war can be. This was savage and violent, and I lost the naive idealism I had when I first went into the Army.

I have now seen quite a bit of ethnic cleansing and genocide in my life. I wouldn't have chosen to, but there you are, that's the way it has gone, and I have to say I am continually shocked by our capacity as a species to inflict suffering on each other. But one tour changed my life: Rwanda. Coping with the aftermath of genocide made me utterly convinced of the physicality of evil. You could touch, taste and feel it.

Around about the spring of 1994, we began to see reports of things going on in Rwanda. What was unfolding before our eyes was the size of the tragedy. There were roughly eight million people living in Rwanda before the war and within a few months, that was down to just over four million. Rwanda was the biggest proportionate per capita genocide the world has ever seen. My brigade was the quick reaction brigade, so you always kept your eye on what was going on in the rest of the world, and we began to think, Now, what does that mean for us?

We were finally warned off at the end of June. In essence, a warning order gives an initial stab at time frame, anticipated force levels and capabilities within that level. We were told to assemble a force of about six hundred as part of UNAMIR (United Nations Assistance Mission for Rwanda) 2, the enhanced UN military force in Rwanda.

The next debate to be had was about the six hundred guys. OK, which guys?

We had three competing sets of priorities – which doesn't necessarily help when you are defining what components to take. According to Whitehall, the priority was 'engineering, logistics, medical'. From the UN in New York, we got 'logistics, engineering, medical', and from General Dallaire, the commander on the ground in Rwanda, we received a communication: 'No, no, no. It's medical, engineering, logistics.'

In the end, we took a squadron from the Royal Engineers – very, very useful blokes to have to build bridges, roads, culverts and all that sort of stuff. We took some logisticians from the Royal Logistic Corps to help with the movement of kit, people and transport, and a small element of electrical and mechanical Engineers from REME to make sure everything worked. Clearly, we needed some communicators to make sure we would get comms links within the country and back to UK, so some Royal Corps of Signals went. We also took a small element, literally a platoon, with a company headquarters, of infantry because the security threat wasn't judged to be that bad. Finally, I took about 150 guys from my unit, which included a field surgical team with complete operating capability, a psychiatrist and a handful of GPs, about twelve of them, plus some nursing officers and paramedics.

We had to wear the UN blue beret, which was difficult: bear in mind, we were paratroopers and to give up our red beret was quite a sense of loss. Actually, we all brought our red berets with us and stashed them in our kit, and wore them on 17 September, which is the day that commemorates the start of the Battle of Arnhem.

We flew into Kigali. I have been to Africa a number of times before, and on all my other African experiences you land in a big city and it's bustling and colourful and noisy. Here was a stunned apathy. The people were almost catatonic. The scale of the disaster was so enormous, everybody had been touched by this genocide – they had perpetrated it, witnessed it or members of their family or their community had been victims of it – and it hung like a black pall over everything you saw or did.

I was met by my operations officer, who took me straight away to our British headquarters, which was in the old sports stadium. The British commander was a chum of mine, Mike Wharmby, a smashing bloke; we were lieutenant colonels together, so we knew each other pretty well. 'You took your time getting here,' was the first thing he said, but as I chatted to Mike, I got the information as to what was going on in the country.

It was mayhem. The Hutu government, which had overseen the genocide, had fled into Zaire and the Tutsis, who had won the war, hadn't yet formed an administration. There was a complete power vacuum while they were organising themselves, leaving a country that had no infrastructure, no social fabric, no courts, no judiciary, no police force. Plus there had been massive migration of nearly two million people, a cholera epidemic, and fighting and genocide were still happening.

I went to the UN headquarters about a mile down the road and met General Dallaire, who was French Canadian and a paratrooper. He had forecast this genocide and had warned the UN Security Council, but his warnings had been ignored and that weighed heavily on his mind because he cared deeply for Rwanda. I warmed to this man immediately, I thought he was a really good bloke, but he was hurting, and, I would say, he was very, very tired.

Like all UN Forces, the Force in Rwanda was a mix of people, some of whom were extremely competent and those who were less so. The Australians sent a field hospital, which stayed within the capital city Kigali, and they were very effective, absolutely excellent. The Canadians sent a signal battalion and one or two others, and were very good; the Canadians always are. And then you got a collection of African units, mainly infantry, and Asian units, who, shall we say, have a different military culture.

Let me give you an example. A BBC wildlife unit from Bristol came to film the Rwandan mountain gorillas. Very nice bunch of people. They wanted to record the effect of the war on this threatened community. They asked about the security situation up in the volcanoes and the mountains where the gorillas were. I rang up the unit headquarters in Kigali and said, 'Can I have intelligence for mines and will you tell me what's happening with the insurgent pattern of conflict in this area?' I got a reply from a Bangladeshi staff officer: 'There are no mines and no more fighting, it's all moved off.' OK. So off they went, this team from Bristol. They had been gone about eight hours when I received a phone call from a British officer at the UN headquarters to say he had just seen my request for information. Did I know that this area was heavily mined and they had intelligence of at least four Hutu groups active in the area? It was too late to stop the camera crew – they were now well up the mountain in the jungle. This caused me a few sleepless nights, I can tell you. Every time there was a bang over the next few days, I'd be thinking, Oh my goodness what's happened now? Mercifully, they came down after four or five days, delighted with what they had filmed. But for me it was an early introduction into working with a UN headquarters. You have to check, cross check and double check everything.

Another example. Nobody had got an overview, so no one could tell me where all the refugee camps were and what the access routes were like. I spent the first week splitting my men into small recce units to go and find them all, map them and do an assessment of access, because this is mountainous terrain. There's water running off the mountains and we knew the wet season was a matter of a few weeks away, and that would change a dirt track into all sorts of problems. By the end of the week, we got a map up on the wall that showed where all the camps were, plus assessments of them, and then we put in the Engineers to do culvert repairs, track repairs and bridge operations in order to guarantee access.

While working on this task I saw my first massacre site. There were four of us in a Land Rover on a recce group I was leading. As we went around a corner, you could see about fifteen thousand makeshift shelters covering the hillside, down the valley and up to the road – the displaced population were very good at making these things with branches and leaves, and provided the foliage was fresh, they would be windproof and rainproof. The UN estimated four people would live in each one, which gives you a population of around sixty thousand. Nobody was there. More importantly, as we looked around, we could see that cooking pots had been abandoned, which is a very bad prognosticator because most of these people lived on sorghum beans which need cooking, you can't eat that stuff raw.

We went to the church. Many Tutsis and moderate Hutus, particularly in rural areas, had fled to their churches in search of sanctuary – and many of them were murdered in those churches. Some priests had been saintly in trying to defend that community and indeed were themselves murdered, but I think some priests had personal failings there. We walked in – and found ourselves ankle deep in the remains of people who had been murdered. They had clearly been macheted; you could see from the marks on the skull and around the neck. It looked like grenades and machine guns had been used as well. The corpses were in advanced degrees of decomposition because when you're hard up against the Equator, flesh doesn't stay around too long, but the truth is, these disasters are always disproportionately visited upon the more vulnerable elements of societies and that tends to be women, particularly pregnant and lactating women, the young and the elderly.

It was really quite unsettling.

34

No one said a word. We walked around in complete silence. We then withdrew from the massacre site and went back to the vehicle. It must have been an hour before anyone could speak. Eventually, I radioed the co-ordinates into regional headquarters and waited for the UN to come out – this was now a war crimes site, so forensically it had to be preserved for the War Crimes Investigation Team.

When you see things like that, you realise how flawed we are as a species. For me that was a personal Rubicon. I found it profoundly, psychologically dislocating, and it is one of those things I recognise has changed me. I do apologise if I sound a bit pious, but when you have seen such things, I don't think you can ever be the same again.

Later on that day, one of my groups radioed in that they had found an orphanage with about a hundred kids and it was in bad order. We happened to be about five kilometres away, so went to see it. It was terrible. All the adults had gone. When we arrived a kid had just died and some of the children were digging a grave outside. We went into this single-storey, white building, and human faeces flowed over the welts of our boots. You can't walk away from that – these kids were going to die if we didn't do something. We put in an environmental health team, a medical team and an engineer team, to sort it out, and then we worked with Care Australia, an excellent NGO, which came and looked after the orphanage. Eventually, they took the orphans to a bigger, established orphanage because you need specialised skills for contact tracing and adoption programmes.

Up in a place called Ruhengeri, about twenty-five kilometres from the Zaire border, we found a hospital that had been built as a barracks by the French Foreign Legion about twenty years before. It had been knocked about, but hadn't been trashed, so we moved in and got the thing working again. We had a treatment facility within twenty-four hours, using surgical teams and all our medical staff, and then continued to improve it. The hospital worked well – in ten days we treated around about six thousand people.

On Sunday of each week I instituted a series of audits to look at all the patients we had treated and try to evaluate what diseases there were. About half were enteric – dysentery, that sort of stuff – and then you had cholera and malaria, which are endemic. Then measles and meningitis, which tend to take the young, the four- to sixteen-year-olds, and finally, respiratory, which tends to affect all groups, but particularly the elderly.

Of all those diseases, for me cholera was the worst one to see because if you have a bad case, your patient can be fine in the morning and dead at night. All the liquid in a person just runs out of the gut. It's classically called rice-water stools. We improvised a cholera cot. We removed some of the springs out of the middle of a standard hospital bed, making a little tunnel in the middle, and put the patient's rectum over that. Initially, we put bed pans underneath, but they weren't very good because the pan would be full in minutes. We then went up in size to a bucket and in the end we used bins; you can imagine how unpleasant it was constantly running out with these bins full of stools, in a small, confined area, with no air conditioning.

Goma was a refugee camp at the northern end of Lake Kivu at the end of the Great Rift Valley in Zaire. It was a terrible business too, a million and a half people thrown together on a volcanic plateau. It just went on and on as far as the eye could see.

At the top end of that plateau, about ten, fifteen kilometres away, was a ring of volcanoes. While I was there, one of the volcanoes began to smoke and one thought, Oh no, how can an extinct volcano decide to erupt now? This is just biblical proportions stuff.

Mercifully, it smoked for about five days and then stopped.

On a volcanic plateau you've got two feet of intensely fertile soil that you can grow anything on but underneath there is hard volcanic rock. You can't dig drains, certainly with what is available to you as a displaced person – you need explosives and heavy plant to do that. As a consequence, all the human debris of Goma got washed into Lake Kivu, the water source, so you got this terrible cholera cycle.

In Rwanda I insisted that if you treated a refugee and sadly that refugee died, you went to the funeral. That wasn't very popular initially, but I think by the end of the deployment our people became aware it was a very good way to ensure that you never became so hardened or inured to distress, misery and hardship that you lost sight of the fact that these are personal tragedies. I believe you need to keep sight of the individual in order to retain your humanity.

Coming home after something like that is difficult. Being back in England is a bit like *Alice Through the Looking-Glass* because everything is familiar, but different. Because you are different. It is really nice to be back home and yet at the same time you have left a part of you behind. Also you need to be given a bit of time and space to make sense of an extraordinary set of experiences, to put them into context.

37

Many of my boys got irritated with that mundane, banal sort of stuff like school fees or the mortgage. I reacted the other way. I thought, Thank God that's all I've got to worry about. But it took time to heal, and a couple of the lads didn't make it.

I lost two soldiers afterwards to post-traumatic stress disorder (PTSD). We also lost two sappers to mines. Now that was probably a price worth paying for what was achieved, but there ain't such a thing as a cost-free operation. We have to understand that there is a human cost to pay every time you deploy people on such operations.

We had two videos in camp. One was the film *Tombstone*, the story of Wyatt Earp and the shoot-out at the O.K. Corral, which I bought at the end of the tour even though by then I knew every single word. The other one, now my favourite film, was *Zulu*.

There is a scene where the two lieutenants, Chard and Bromhead, played by Michael Caine and Stanley Baker, are standing in the burned-out remains of a hospital. Neither of them had ever fought in action before and Chard says to Bromhead: 'Well, you fought your first action, how do you feel?' Bromhead replies: 'I'm tired, I'm tired to my bones . . . And there is something more than that. I'm ashamed.'

I absolutely agree with that. That one little scene in *Zulu* summed it all up entirely. We were dog tired because we treated something like 136,000 patients, built 18 bridges, repaired 70-odd culverts, moved 80,000 people, shifted 6000 tons of food, did an awful lot, without a day off really – you just cracked on because the need was overwhelming, but God you were tired.

I was a little ashamed too. I was a child of the sixties, but the optimism and idealism that we could change the world was tempered by hard experience in Northern Ireland, Bosnia, Kosovo, Sierra Leone and also the Afghanistan and Iraq experiences. I have witnessed obscenity, bigotry and prejudice taken to extremes, as in Rwanda, resulting in genocide, murder, intimidation and ethnic cleansing. Equally, there have been shining examples of courage and integrity. I think I now have a balanced view of humankind. People are people. They are a bewildering and beguiling combination of strength and weakness.

LANCE CORPORAL CALLUM MACKENZIE

'Thanks to Laura ...'

I am from a small town in Wiltshire where there is not really that much to do. It's either a case of stacking shelves in Sainsbury's or getting away from there and doing something with your life. I chose Option B. I joined the Army at sixteen, straight from school.

I had my heart set on going to an engineering regiment and I did the combat engineers' course. It was one of the hardest things I've done in my life. After I completed it I was found to be colour blind and told by the CO that I couldn't stay. I was mortified. That was the ultimate kick in the teeth. Instead of getting posted to one of the engineering regiments, they advised me to look at something within the Royal Logistic Corps. My options were driver, postie or seaman/navigator. Not being a driver, and getting seasick, I thought, I'll see what postie is like.

I did the Postal and Courier Operator Class 3 training at Deepcut and I saw that posties come in all different shapes, colours, creeds, nationalities and religions. I work with Fijian

40

guys, massive big fellas who love playing rugby, little three-foot-tall Nepalese blokes transferred from the Royal Gurkha Rifles, fat Welsh blokes and skinny Scottish people. But the one thing we have in common is that we're all very hard working.

I was deployed to Iraq on Operation Telic 9 and arrived there six weeks after my eighteenth birthday. I had never been any-where like Iraq – I think the sunniest place I'd been until then was Cornwall.

The first night in Iraq was a bit of an eye opener. We had a mortar rocket attack. I wasn't used to the heat and had woken up in the middle of the night and was trying to get back to sleep, when I heard a massive bang. I lay there, thinking, Oh, what's this? One of the guys rolled off his camp cot and said to me, 'Mate, have you been to Iraq before? I think you ought to lie on the floor.' I spent an hour on the floor and then thought, Sod this, and got back into bed.

I was working in the central distribution office, basically where all the mail comes in from the UK. Our job was to provide postal support to all the in-theatre regiments and brigades. We were doing twelve-hour shifts, but everything started to get a lot busier in the run-up to Christmas. Some days we were working sixteen, seventeen hours, cracking through upwards of two thou-sand bags every night shift, which is quite a lot of mail between eight people.

The beginning of February, one of the sergeants in my squadron said, 'You're going down to the Shatt-al-Arab Hotel to replace one of the guys who's going on his R & R.' I was meant to go on a helicopter flight, but that was cancelled due to bad weather, so the next day I went out on the road with the guys from the 1st Battalion Staffordshire Regiment. I spent two hours before we left cleaning and prepping my rifle for firing, if need be. That was a big experience, sitting in the back of the Warrior with a bunch of sweaty infantry blokes. I was eager and a bit wary at the same time. After about an hour, there was an IDF (indirect fire) attack, just metres away, which was a bit of a wake-up call.

The post office in the Shatt was a tiny little room, but we were very busy, working really long hours. Before we'd gone out, we had been told: 'Either you'll be a person who's happy sat in the post office doing sod all, other than stamping a couple of letters, or you'll be proactive and try to help the guys as much as you can.' Obviously, all posties I know are in the second category! I would finish sorting at three or four in the morning and then help the chefs clean up pots and pans or help the guys in motor transport refuel a vehicle – just little things like that, but making someone else's life a bit easier. The Army's one big team at the end of the day. In turn, guys would come back in off patrols and say, 'Is there any mail for our call sign, any mail for our lads?' and then give me a hand in the post office.

Well, I was quite lucky because in that post office we had a military phone from which you could dial out and use your welfare phone calls. I used to phone Laura in the middle of the night – Laura's from the same town as me, we were courting at the time. And whether it be five in the morning or ten at night, she always answered the phone, which was really good. She gave me loads of moral support – which I needed. Being a postie is not the most dangerous job in the world, particularly when you think of guys out on patrol, getting shot at and blown up every day, and I was beginning to feel like I wasn't that important. However, talking to Laura made me realise what I was doing was very worthwhile. The guys coming off strike ops at four in the morning, all sweaty after being in contact for a couple of hours: chuck them a parcel from home full of chocolates or Haribos or Pot Noodles and they really appreciate it. Something as simple as a bluey with three little words in it, 'I love you', from the wife or girlfriend can give someone so much more energy and optimism. Thanks to Laura, when I thought about it in those terms, I began to find real job satisfaction.

After being at the Shatt for three weeks, I phoned Laura up one day and said, 'I'm going to marry you.'

'Oh, OK,' she said. 'What's brought this on?'

And I said, 'Well, not trying to be pessimistic or anything, but you don't know what life is going to bring.' I suppose it was a bit of an unromantic proposal, and I got a bit of grief off Laura for that later. But we did it, we got married after I came back off tour. We have got a little boy, Kieran, who's just turned one, and she's pregnant again. Actually, she's due this week.

I know this might sound really harsh, but after I came back from Iraq I severed ties with a lot of my civvy friends. There is this one lad I went to school with, he'd been a good mate of mine for five or six years. Before I left, he was sat on his arse in his mum's front room playing computer games, smoking fags and drinking beer. Came back from Iraq and he was still sat in the same spot, smoking fags, drinking the same cans of beer.

Also, I've got a younger brother who is a bit of a tearaway, so me and him don't see eye to eye. But I have spoken to him a couple of times: 'Instead of wasting your life, why don't you think about joining the Forces?' and he's told me he'll think about it, which I am happy about. I like to think maybe I've given him a little example. But the thing that has surprised me most is that my little sister, who's the most intellectually gifted out of the three of us – she's level-pegging for genius – she said, 'I'm going to join the Army when I've finished my college courses.' Fair play to her, I'm really proud.

We have had quite a long break between deployments. The squadron I'm part of at the moment are due to deploy to Afghanistan later this year, which is good, although it will be strange leaving my family. But Laura is married to the Army as much as I am. If I've got to go away, she'll take it in her stride.

MAJOR PAURIC NEWLAND

'Maytaanayn daroun byaayaym ou az shumaa chand sawaal kounayn?'

I'm a linguist and help train soldiers to speak foreign languages on operations, plus promote cultural awareness – understanding the environment they're operating in. We are bashing up against the indigenous population on operations, and no matter how wonderful it is for us to be helping them and all that, we are fighting wars in their countries and we must try to respect their values, their architecture, their history. So while our soldiers are patrolling and meeting the civ-pop, we train them to act a certain way in order to show respect – 'gaining hearts and minds' is the old terminology for it.

For example, there are slightly different methods of greeting out there. Say you are going to talk to a village elder in Afghanistan. You would put your hand on your heart, make lots of eye contact and give a big firm handshake that would last a lot longer than the usual UK handshake – they're quite touchy-feely in the Arab world when it comes to initial greetings and men holding hands is not seen as anything particularly strange. We also teach soldiers about their houses: to you and me it may look like a mud hut, but that might be the local mosque and you have to treat it completely differently. In houses you have prayer rooms that don't look different from any other room, but we have to respect those rooms a little bit more.

If we are entering a home on a soft knock, say searching for IEDs, we would teach our soldiers to ask permission first and always go to the eldest male in the house and not talk to any women. We wouldn't say, 'Everyone in the house get in one room.' We would go to the clear leader of the house and say, 'Please can we come in and ask you some questions?' *Maytaanayn daroun byaayaym ou az shumaa chand sawaal kounayn?* Now, we don't need their permission to do these things, and if he doesn't give permission, we are still going in – sometimes we have to blow doors down or kick them in, things like that.

We try to give the soldiers a general awareness about the hierarchies in villages and tribes. Societies like these are very much about rank. In Iraq there will be a hereditary tribal leader, a sheikh of some sort, and his position would be based on inheritance and family. In Afghanistan, people can lose their position in the hierarchy if they fail to deliver the goods: it is what you can provide for your tribe that maintains you in power, so the guy has to be successful at getting things – money, land, livestock – otherwise he can be usurped.

The soldier gets a language card that has a few hundred words and phrases on it. We wouldn't expect the soldier on the ground to master a foreign language. For one thing, Pashtu, which is mainly used in Helmand, is very difficult. It's got something like forty-two letters in the alphabet and seems to have no real agreement on grammatical structure. Fortunately, the Afghan National Army and the police use Dari, which is based on Farsi, and it does have a structure, so if we are in a mentoring role, then that's what we use.

My department employs LECs, local employed civilians. They are quite well paid in a place where unemployment is very high, but it is a dangerous job, and you risk getting killed for doing it. People were literally being picked up off the streets and shot by the insurgents for having anything to do with the British.

We are very careful with our LECs. If one dies, we take great pains with the handing back of the body. For example, an interpreter working with a battle group out in the desert was on a vehicle that was chasing an insurgent vehicle in a gun battle. The vehicle rolled and he was crushed, and then helicoptered back to the COB (contingency operating base).

We didn't know his real name, nor did any of his fellow interpreters, so we couldn't ring his family. One of the interpreters scrolled through his mobile phone, found a number that looked like a dad or brother and rang them up. We finally got his older brother, told him what had happened, and arranged a time to meet outside the gate of the COB to hand over the body. We had to do it as subtly as possible because the family would not want to be seen going into the British base, nor would they want anybody to know that one of their family was working for us.

Eventually, something like a Volkswagen Camper Van pulled up and nine balaclavared people got out. I thought to myself, I shouldn't really be here on my own, this is an orange jumpsuit moment. I was just hoping that the guard on the tower was looking through his telescopic sights and if anything happened that he would start shooting. But it was the real family. They had covered up so no one would see them coming on to a British Army base.

They were very emotional, lots of crying and wailing and beating themselves, asking stuff like, 'Why, oh why?' And then, finally, they did the 'It's God's will' bit. When they had calmed down, we explained what had happened, through the interpreter, and that we would pay them for his death in service, which would be cash in hand. To them that would be a perfectly normal way to go about things, even though that sounds quite strange to us.

I was not very religious before I went to Iraq and Afghanistan. I am even less religious now, not because of the death and destruction I saw in battle, but I just find religions and belief in God ultimately inhibits humans. For example, there is this Arab term, *inshallah*, if God wills it. Some people might say, 'Well, that's very pious, you are opening yourself to God controlling your life.' But it can really hinder progress. Say there's a well that is poisoned and the water is shit. Rather than dig a new well, they will accept being poisoned by the water, '*Inshallah*. God wills that I'm going to get poisoned.' They will do stupid stuff in a firefight like stand up in open ground to fire at you. '*Inshallah*. If God wills it, I'm going to die.' Well, you are going to die, mate, because you're standing up. If you just stayed laid down, you wouldn't.

When I came back from Iraq, I was of a mind that some things don't matter as much as people think they do. For example, my parents used to have a newspaper shop and, to some people, especially retired people, getting their copy of the *Daily Telegraph* in the morning was the most important thing in the world. If it had run out, that was a major tragedy in their life. You can see how ridiculous that is compared with the sort of things that happen to the average Iraqi, who is worrying about getting enough water and food and having enough clothes to wear. Somehow people here see those trivialities as important and that's because the important things are already covered, you know – they are clothed, they are fed, they have everything covered.

I am amazed that little bits of Iraq and Afghanistan have entered my soul, snuck their way in, because if you asked me what those countries are like, they're shit holes. What's Afghanistan like? It's a shit hole. So is Iraq. I wouldn't live there if you paid me. But then sometimes you remember sunsets and nights when it's all warm, and you can hear the wind blowing through the few trees there are, and it is deeply still and quiet. Moments like that are beautiful and they remain with you.

LANCE CORPORAL MICHELLE NORRIS

'A pretty difficult manoeuvre in the number-two skirt...'

We medics can adapt to different situations. We can work in medical centres or in hospitals, whether that be surgical wards or emergency departments. We can also be on the frontline with the soldiers as a first responder and we're there to deliver emergency first aid at the point of wounding.

I went to Germany for my first posting. I had been there for six months and one afternoon on parade one of the sergeants said, 'Right, we need six volunteers to go to Iraq on Telic 6.' I looked around at a couple of my mates and we nodded at each other as if to say, 'Right, let's go.'

And that was it, we were off. I was told I was to be attached to the 1st Battalion Princess of Wales's Royal Regiment (PWRR). We flew from Hanover on a civilian flight into Kuwait, took a Herc into Al Amarah, and got put straight away into QRF, which is the quick reaction force. First operation was just a normal patrol around Al Amarah town in the back of a Warrior, but when I stepped foot out on the ground with my rifle cocked and loaded, I was like, Wow, yeah, this is the real deal – I'm a proper soldier now.

We were constantly out and about trying to locate weapon caches and things like that. We were contacted a couple of times, which was pretty scary, and we also hit an IED in a Warrior one day and the back filled up with smoke. You had that split second to wonder, 'Oh my God, is this it?' But then because we're trained to brush it off, we just got on with the job.

The 11th of June 2006 was a major operation in which the whole battle group was involved: the light infantry, the Royal Engineers, the Queen's Royal Hussars and aspects of the artillery. We all went out to different places to try and find things. I was with Company HQ of PWRR. I had a headset on, so could hear different radio reports, and there were a lot of contacts out on the ground. In the early hours of the morning we heard that a Warrior had got bogged down in a ditch, and received a report to go to that area because a crowd was gathering.

As we got there, I could hear these dings coming off our Warrior. Then I heard the turret get hit, where the gunner and the commander sit. I shouted out, 'Is everyone all right?' There was no answer, but I could still see movement of their legs above me, so I assumed everything must be fine and it was just stones hitting us, because we'd been stoned before. Right at that point, the gunner shouted down to me, 'Chuck [my nickname], Page has been hit, Page has been hit.' I looked up and could see Pagey slumped on the floor in the turret, although I couldn't see his injuries.

Colour Sergeant Ian Page. He was the quartermaster for C

Company and a brilliant man. When it was his birthday out there, I asked him how old he was. It turned out he was forty odd and I said, 'You're old enough to be my dad', because I was only eighteen at the time. 'You cheeky so and so,' he replied. Ever since then I started calling him 'Dad' and he was calling me 'Daughter'. We'd make each other cups of tea, and just really got on well, always having a laugh together.

The lads in the back tried to get the turret cage open, so they could bring in Page, but it was stuck. I thought, Right, I can't leave him there because what if he's really seriously injured? I told the driver to stop the vehicle and I jumped out of the back and climbed on to the top of the Warrior to assess the situation. I wasn't aware of anything going on around me. I didn't even realise I was getting shot at. When I looked down at Pagey, I could see he had a massive hole in his face.

'Right, get my med bergen up here,' I shouted, but at that moment the lads managed to open the turret cage inside and pushed him through. The gunner, Private Ratawake, a Fijian and a good friend of mine, grabbed me by my collar and literally dragged me head first back into the Warrior.

We stretched Pagey out on the floor and the guys pushed up as much as they could because it's quite cramped in the back of a Warrior. I began treating Page as we were moving. I checked his vital signs, his pulse, his blood pressure and his breathing. There was not a lot of light, so we opened the top cover to let in some of the sunlight. I also used my pen torch to look into his eyes to see if there was any damage, and I had to undress him and check everywhere else. Although he had lost a lot of blood, he was talking, so I knew he was fine. I asked if there was any pain

anywhere else and he said, 'No.' I went to give him IV fluids and
he pulled away. 'No, I don't want anything.' He had been shot
in the face. There could have been head injuries, or anything, so
you can't give morphine in those situations. It would make him
drowsy and affect his pupils which would hinder assessment
of any raised intracranial pressure. So there was really nothing
I could do apart from stop the bleeding with a normal field
dressing and try to get him as comfortable as possible – which
probably wasn't too comfortable, driving at speed in the back of
a Warrior, going over bumps, and being fired at.

Finally, we arrived at the HLS, so he could be evacuated. The
lads got him on to the stretcher and just before we put him into
the helicopter, I got hold of his hand and gave it a little bit of
a squeeze. Then it was back into the Warrior and carry on with
the task.

We eventually got back to camp and as we parked up and
unloaded our weapons, the sergeant major came over to me,
shook my hand and said, 'What you did today was absolutely brilliant. You'll probably get an MiD for that.' I didn't
know what that was, but one of the guys explained it to me:
'Mentioned in Dispatches'. I said, 'OK, that would be pretty
cool', although I didn't do it to get a medal or anything like
that.

Also, I had already begun to worry: Gosh, what if I had got
something wrong? What about his wife, and his mum and dad
and his family? But then someone at the hospital in Shaiba
phoned, asking to speak to me. He said, 'Other medics would
have done this and that, someone might have put a neck collar
on, which would have caused more complications, but you didn't

go overboard, you just kept it basic and you saved his life.' And I thought, Hmm, not doing a lot is sometimes better.

When I returned to Iraq after R & R, the sergeant major printed off a news article from the internet. At the bottom of the article it said, 'She'll probably be getting a Military Cross.' I went straight over to phone my mum. I got through and had just begun, 'Hello Mum, I've got something to tell you. . .' when she started in at me: 'Michelle, do you know how much hassle you've caused me? I've got reporters from all over the country knocking on my door.' It turns out my story had gone everywhere. I couldn't believe it.

All the newspapers got little bits wrong in their own ways. One said I had been shot through the rucksack, which I never had – the only thing that got shot was a radio next to my knee on top of the turret. I didn't have my bergen on my back, nor did I have my rifle in my hand. But the thing that really got to me, because I am very proud of my corps, was they all kept writing 'The Royal Armoured Medical Corps', when it's 'The Royal *Army* Medical Corps'. It didn't matter how many times I told them, they would still get it wrong.

There were always more interviews to do and in the end I just wanted to chill out and be left alone. I don't like being the centre of attention because I know tons of people who have done a lot more than I have and don't get recognised for it.

I didn't see Pagey until we came back to Germany from the tour. We had to hand in our body armour and as we walked towards the stores, I thought I could hear him. I said, 'Is that Pagey?' and people were going, 'Yeah, yeah, you've got to talk to him.' As I walked in, he said, 'Ah, Private Norris, come here.' He put down his clipboard and his papers and just gave me a massive hug. He said, 'Thank you very much, I owe you one.'

I said, 'I was only doing my job', and he said, 'No, you did outstanding, thank you.' Obviously he looked better than when I last saw him, but he had a lot of swelling because he'd had a lot of surgery – it looked like someone had stuck a tennis ball on the side of his face. But he looked fine otherwise and he has got better ever since.

I was pretty much flown straight away back to London, where a lot of servicemen and I were told what awards we were going to receive. My citation was read out, and I was told I was to receive the Military Cross. At that moment the 2iC came up to me and said, 'You do realise you're the first female ever to receive the MC?' I was absolutely gobsmacked that I was going down in history. I didn't know what to say or do!

My family came down from Stourbridge for the awards. At that time I was on a Class 1 course at Keogh Barracks, so they drove down to Aldershot and we all took the train to London together. When we got to Buckingham Palace, my mum, dad and sister had to go into a room where I was going to be presented with the medal. The rest of us getting awards went upstairs. All kinds of people were getting medals that day: military, police, fire service, oh, and Stevie Gerrard, the footballer was there.

Before we went in to see the Queen, we were taught how to curtsey properly by this rather posh lady. Just as well, though, as I'd never curtseyed before. 'Just put your right leg behind your left leg and bend down holding your skirt,' she said, which is a pretty difficult manoeuvre in the number-two skirt, let me tell you. There were quite a lot of laughs while we were all learning that and one or two had a bit of a tumble, although in the end everyone got it right.

Then, all of a sudden, it was, 'Private Norris, come through.' I went round the corner and, like, oh my God, there's the Queen, and before I knew it, I was standing in front of her. How mad is that?

I threw a curtsey and went, 'Hello, Your Majesty.' And she said, 'Hello, I'm very pleased to be giving you this award today, your family must be extremely proud.'

'They are ma'am,' I said. 'They're in the audience.'

She said, 'Where are you based now?'

'In Germany,' I said, and she asked whether I was going back out to Iraq, and I said, 'Yes, at the end of the year with my unit.'

'Well,' she said, 'I wish you all the luck and happiness in the world. Just keep safe.' Then she leaned over and hooked on my medal, which has a purple and white ribbon on the top and a silver cross with my name engraved on the back. And that was it. She was absolutely brilliant. I curtseyed again, turned to the right and walked off.

We had photographs taken in the courtyard and some more interviews to do, and then we went back to the hotel room and had something to eat. And after that I had to get back to barracks because the next afternoon I had an exam to take – which I passed!

LANCE CORPORAL MICHELLE NORRIS

Official citation accompanying Military Cross for Private Michelle Norris, Royal Army Medical Corps

At just 19 years of age and having only recently completed basic training, Private Michelle Norris was deployed as a medical orderly with The Queen's Royal Hussars Battle Group in Al Amarah, Southern Iraq. 11 June 2006 saw the largest and most intense battle in Iraq since 2004. A search operation in Al Amarah turned into a war-fighting engagement when her Company Group came under heavy, accurate and sustained attack from a well-organised enemy force of over 200.

During the heaviest of the fighting the company commander's group came under accurate sniper fire and the commander of the Warrior carrying Private Norris was shot in the face and seriously injured. Private Norris realised the severity of the situation immediately and without thought or care for her own personal safety, dismounted and climbed onto the top of the Warrior to administer life-saving first aid to the casualty. On seeing her on the top of the Warrior the sniper opened fire again, firing a further three rounds at her, one hitting the radio mounted on the side of the turret inches from her leg. Despite this she continued to administer first aid through the commander's hatch to the casualty until the gunner pulled her into the turret for her own safety.

Despite the very real risks from sniper fire, heavy small arms fire and rocket propelled grenade she deliberately ignored the danger to her own life in order to administer life-saving first aid to the commander of the vehicle. Private Norris's actions on 11 June were extremely courageous and outstandingly brave and have rightly earned her the Military Cross for actions to save the life of a comrade when under fire.

LIEUTENANT COLONEL KEN ROBERTS

'A hierarchy of importance...'

I was in northern Iraq just after the first Gulf War with the Kurdish relief operation and it was a very strange deployment to be involved in. Everybody was coming home from the Gulf, when the then Prime Minister, John Major, decided it would be a good idea for us to help these poor Kurds.

We were trying to deploy while everybody else was coming back. I had to draw a team from eight different locations in the UK and Germany, plus get all the kit and vehicles when most of it was in the Gulf, and put it together in about a week, which was quite a challenge. Having got there, we were working with people we had never worked with before, like 3 Commando Brigade and the Royal Marines, who didn't understand who the hell we were because they didn't have any environmental heath guys.

It took a while for them to work out what we could do for them and then for us to discover the way they did their business. Initially, we were told our role was merely to support the brigade, but then it became pretty apparent that we could be quite effective in looking after the health of some of the refugees, and so our main effort changed quite quickly.

None of us had ever been involved with large numbers of refugees before – we are talking about tens of thousands here – and we found that quite a challenge, I have to say.

We originally worked in a place called Silopi, which is in the middle of a large, horrible, dusty plain on the Turkish–Iraqi border. The Iraqi military were just heading away. They had deliberately and maliciously destroyed everything in their wake. They smashed up hospitals and fouled the rooms by defecating all over the place, conduct I found fairly difficult to accept from what was purportedly an army. We went into Zakho, a border town in Iraq, just across from Silopi, and found the water treatment plant had been smashed. They destroyed any utility they could find. You could see it wasn't done for any military reasons – we weren't going to be using that infrastructure for ourselves – so it was almost like a punishment to the Kurds for daring to have a resistance. I was very angered by what the Iraqis did because it was sheer bloody-minded vandalism.

We flew up to the hills where many of the refugees had ended up: they had plonked themselves down in vast areas that were pretty well unsupportable – nowhere near rivers, for example, so we were having to tanker water in, which was a complete logistical nightmare.

They had been up in the hills for a long time and they weren't used to living rough – a lot of these people weren't country dwellers, but sophisticated, urbanised people. They had left in a hurry, so most of them didn't have an awful lot of stuff with them. They had been exposed to the elements and were exhausted, hungry and dehydrated. Lots were suffering from diarrhoeal disease because they couldn't wash and we began to see people with lice and things like that.

People were suffering clinically from cholera and, as usual, the ones most affected were the very young and the very old. A child will die of cholera in a day. Seeing these kids just fading away before your very eyes was quite difficult to live with. It was shocking, actually. At that time my two daughters were seven and five, so you can imagine how it made me feel.

We were very lucky in that we had a Navy paediatrician with us and also a number of naval midwives who were fantastic with the children. But really, when you are dealing with that number of people, it is pretty difficult to do any meaningful stuff. You knew in your heart there was nothing you could do for them because they were too far gone, so our role was to try to reduce the threat for the next lot, as it were.

We set up decent, very formalised camps down on the Zakho Plain. They were nicely tented. We had safe water and decent food supplies, medical cover as well, so we could actually look at their medical needs when they got there. But an awful lot of them wanted to go home as opposed to going to a camp, which is quite reasonable. These people were terrified, convinced they were all going to be killed by the Iraqis.

Then we got this call: 'The operation's over, your team is going home tomorrow, somebody else is going to do it now.' We had to disengage overnight from people we had been working with and I was home within twenty-four hours of leaving the refugee camp.

Everyone thought they were doing us a favour to get us home so quickly, but I arrived completely confused and tired after the whole thing.

Also, everyone expects that somehow you will just miraculously adjust, but it took me some considerable time to recover. No matter how professionally detached you try to be, you do get an attachment to people, and we had been living cheek by jowl in fairly rough conditions with the refugees for several weeks. We had seen some pretty horrible things during that time and got to know some people very well. It was a very emotional experience saying goodbye.

Can you imagine going from living like that to coming back to Britain where suddenly you are thrown back into the banality of everyday family life?

It's the really stupid things that you get annoyed about, things that if you try to put them into a hierarchy of importance, compared with what you have seen, melt into insignificance. Holidays, for example. Someone says, 'We need to book a holiday.' 'Yes, whatever, just book a holiday.' 'Where do you want to go?' 'I don't care . . . just book a holiday. Why am I being burdened with this nonsense?' Nowadays we have this system of decompression for people – we make sure they get all the stress and tension out of their system before they come back home.

I did try to talk to my wife about it – she's a minister. But it is difficult to talk to somebody who hasn't been there. You can paint little bits and give vignettes of things, but it's almost impossible to describe the whole picture.

I didn't sleep properly for months. I had nightmares all the time and I felt quite guilty too because at the back of your mind there was always the feeling that we could have done so much more.

The first six months back I was very short with people. I was walking in town with my wife one day and came upon a good civilian friend of mine. 'Oh Ken,' he said, 'it's good to see you back. It must have been rough out there.' I just spat at him: 'You have no idea what you are talking about,' and walked away. After he left, my wife said, 'Where did that come from? He was just trying to be nice.'

My late maternal grandfather was a regular soldier in the Royal Artillery during the Second World War and he'd had a very rough time in Dunkirk. Having got back to the UK, he was posted to Burma, which was something he never talked about, except with members of his old regiment. It was clear he'd had a terrible time. But for twenty years after, he would wake up in the middle of the night, screaming, having had really bad nightmares. Every time I tried to talk to him about it, he would say, 'It just wasn't very nice,' and that was it, end of conversation. Only when he was dying did we have a chat. I asked him, 'What was Burma like?' And this time he really unloaded. He said, 'I was never going to tell anyone about it because how can you tell anybody?' This whole thing of PTSD never happening to the old boys? Well, that's just not the case. When I asked him why he was telling me now, he said, 'Because you have been through some of this, so you will understand.'

CAPTAIN STEVEN SMALL

'The swing of the kilt . . .'

As a young boy down in the Borders, in Berwickshire, I used to watch the pipe band play and follow behind them all around the town. My brother had started to play the drums, and while they were enrolling him, I wandered next door into the piping classroom and, aged eight, signed up for lessons. I was taught by an old guy called Tim Ainslie, who had served in the Black Watch during the Second World War. He had been injured in the break-out from Tobruk and during his rehabilitation had learned to play the pipes.

Aged sixteen, I joined the Black Watch, and the operational tours I had were all in Northern Ireland during the eighties and nineties. The majority of the time, kids were screaming at you or spitting on you. Doors would close as you passed by. Wherever you went, people would go inside and curtains would be drawn, so it was pretty unpleasant. There were some chinks, like when one old guy gave me a friendly nod, which was just enough to make me think, maybe we are here for the right reasons.

I did three or four different tours of Northern Ireland and in between that went on four three-month tours of America, playing the pipes coast to coast. They always asked for 'Amazing Grace', that's the one they all want to hear. We tried to not include it on the 1998 tour, but that lasted about two shows; it was seen as sacrilege to leave it out. It is a very simple tune and not much of a technical test for a piper, so it becomes pretty mundane. But it can be played in different ways – you need to put it into context. If it is played at a funeral, for example, you have got to slow it down, draw it out and make it a lament. If you are asked to play it at a wedding, you can play it upbeat and lift it up a little bit.

Pipe music is as significant now as it has ever been. You talk to the Jocks – whenever they hear the pipes they will flock towards them. Units coming back from operations are now exercising the right to march through the various towns in their areas, and you will always get the pipes and drums at the front. The troops raise themselves another couple of inches when the pipes start to play. The pipes bring out something within them, their identity, national pride.

The simpler tunes, where the troops can pick up on the melody, are really the best for marching, and give a tempo in which they can get the swing of the kilt and exercise a bit of style. Each unit will have their own particular tunes they identify with: 'Scotland the Brave' is a common regimental tune, and 'Highland Laddie' and 'Black Bear'.

Regimental laments vary from unit to unit. 'Lochaber No More' is one, 'Fingal's Lament' is another, but the majority of regiments have 'Flowers of the Forest' as their funeral march.

It's slow, it has dirge-type qualities, which completely fit a repatriation or funeral-type tune. Plus, it is a lovely tune and very thought-provoking.

I love to play the instrument. I get a lot of satisfaction from it. You need patience, determination and musical knowledge to be a good bagpipe player. But you never master it, there is always room for improvement – my wife encourages me if I am not practising. She is a Highland dancer. She's been dancing ever since a kid and loves the pipes, and our kids love them as well.

The Black Watch were chosen for the last tour of Hong Kong and to close all the military installations in the lead-up to the handover on 1 July. The PLA guys, the People's Liberation Army, from China, came over to Hong Kong and lived in the same camp as us for a wee while. They had obviously sent their biggest, smartest, best English-speaking soldiers across, who were smart and organised, everything you would expect. But they kept themselves to themselves – there wasn't a lot of interaction – although there was a bit of competition in the mornings in the fitness parades to see who was the faster, stronger and bigger – needless to say, the Black Watch always came out on top.

Towards the end of our time in Hong Kong, there were lots of events and ceremonies and beating retreats. I was pipe major at the time and I had pipers all over the place. Then there were rehearsals for the handover parade and they didn't want anything particularly regimental for the final lament. On the evening of the handover everything was going fine, Prince Charles was present, and 750 million were watching on the television. I dropped off to the side in preparation for the final lament and Prince Charles stood up to speak, and as soon as he did, the rains came on – fat, heavy raindrops. It was like being in a shower and I was stood with my pipes on my shoulder, which isn't very good for them.

When I blew the pipes up, some water caused the first note on the F to come out as a flat, horrible sound. I had to clear that first note through. But it went OK after that, although that was a bit of a panic moment.

We came straight off the parade on to boats to the airport, and things went like a well-oiled machine. There were pre-placed boxes at the airport and we went along the line taking off elements of our uniforms and dropping them into the boxes. The boxes were sealed and sent off, and we got changed into our civvies and took off at two minutes to midnight for home. That was our six months done. The kit arrived in Fort George about two months later and, well, wet kilts, shoved dripping into a box, sealed and put on a boat for months . . . let's just say it was not very pleasant opening those boxes. We were on the tattoo that year and we had to get brand-new uniforms for it.

The biggest and most poignant event I have ever played, though, would have been the Queen Mother's funeral. As the senior pipe major on parade at that time – the Black Watch obviously being her regiment – I was the last person to have worn her Pipe Banner on parade.

We were looking so smart for the occasion, wearing our traditional uniform: the ostrich-feather bonnet, of course, with a red hackle; Archer green doublet; Royal Stewart tartan, which was granted by Queen Victoria; the white-hair sporran with five black tassels, significant for the Black Watch, one tassel for each of the original colonels who raised the regiment; the waist belt with the regimental number '42' on the buckle; and the crossbelt with the badge of Scotland and the Black Watch cap badge on it; and red-and-black diced hose, which is the royal pattern; and spats and brogues.

There were thousands and thousands of people lined along the streets outside Westminster Abbey, but there was hardly a sound from them. It was just so sombre and moving. Soldiers had lined the street and were standing in the Recover on the Arms reversed position, which is having their rifles face down and their heads bowed.

We were stood at ease outside and then brought to attention to play while the gun carriage was moved from the Palace of Westminster to Westminster Abbey. We moved as a Massed Pipes and Drums, the drums and the maces all draped in black, and we played 'Mist Covered Mountains' and 'My Home' at seventy-five paces per minute, which is the speed the gun carriage moves.

Then the service took place and as the coffin left Westminster Abbey, we played 'Oft' in the Stilly Night', which is an Irish tune, as the Queen Mother was also Colonel-in-Chief of the Irish Guards. It was a really moving experience.

LANCE CORPORAL LUKE WINTER

'Plenty of cheeky-looking penguins . . .'

I wanted to join the Armed Forces to get away from Doncaster. Nothing wrong with Doncaster – it's just the council estate I was living on had high unemployment and a higher crime rate. You'd hear the sirens from police cars every night and have groups of youths sitting around with cheap bottles of cider doing very little.

I went to the careers office, aged sixteen, resolute about joining the Royal Marines, although I'm not in anyway the shape or form to be a Royal Marine – I'm six foot three, wear glasses and am built pretty much like a beanpole. The Royal Marine recruiter there said, 'Right, jump up on that bar and do heaves until you can't do any more.' And after I did half a dozen, he went, 'Yeah, that's never going to be good enough to join the Royal Marines, maybe you want to consider something less demanding.' I'm not saying the Army's less demanding than the Royal Marines, but it has definitely got a lesser physical-requirement level.

After my abysmal performance, I got some books about

REME, the Royal Electrical and Mechanical Engineers, and I was impressed. It seemed just right for me. I'm technically minded anyway, I have always liked tinkering and taking things to pieces – and the majority of times they would go back together and still operate. I like fixing things. Every broken piece of equipment I pick up is a challenge: 'I've never seen this fault before, let's find out what it is, so I can add it to my repertoire' sort of thing.

But my first priority was to improve on my fitness. The Army target is a mile and a half in under ten minutes and thirty seconds. I started running in the evening when prime-time television was on. Most people were sat glued to their TVs at that time so I was left alone. I got my time down and passed the training course, and was posted to Osnabrück in Germany with the Queen's Royal Lancers as an instruments technician. Basically, if it's got glass in it, I fix it. I fix watches, all kinds of observing devices, like binoculars and telescopes, compasses, thermal-imaging and night-vision goggles. Interestingly enough, I'm a photocopier repairer as well, which I'll tell you about in a moment.

There are some pieces of equipment, like binoculars, which are really difficult to fix. The adjustments are so pernickety and fine, the shake on your hand can take them out. You've got to put more effort into them than other bits of kit that you just slot back together. Compasses and watches are the easiest of all – they are not cost-effective to fix, so once they're broken you chuck them.

We went out on a United Nations tour to Cyprus, where I was fixing telescopes and observing devices and compasses and all the rest of the small glass-faced instruments the Army uses to keep track of what the Greeks and the Turkish are up to.

Then I spent six months doing pre-deployment training for Afghanistan because that is where my unit was going, which I was really excited about. I had even started taking the anti-malaria tablets. On the morning before our flight, I got pulled into the officer commanding's office. 'Stop taking your anti-malaria tablets,' I was told. 'You're not going to Afghanistan, you're going to Altrincham, to do a six-week course on photo-copiers and then out to the Falklands for six months.' It turns out we have a lot of photocopiers on the bases over there and it is more cost-effective for the Army to send military people trained by the company that make the photocopiers, rather than sending over a trained civilian photocopier engineer, which was a shock and a bit of a downer at the time.

So I went to Altrincham in Manchester for a course with Ricoh Photocopiers Ltd to learn how to fix their photocopiers, and then out to the Falklands with another REME technician called Dave McCracken. I'm going to refer to him as Spud because when he introduced himself, it wasn't 'Hi, I'm Dave,' it was 'Hi, I'm Spud.' Really, really good bloke, ginger hair and the attitude to go with it. 'Yes, I'm ginger, what of it?' sort of thing.

We got there in December, which would have been summer for them, although you wouldn't have known, it was that cold. If you took a chunk of Scotland, knocked all the houses down and just let it go rugged for a couple of hundred years, that's the Falklands. It's Scotland, but on the other side of the planet.

Spud and me got given a list of where all the photocopi-ers were, about sixty to seventy of them, and we started going around and finding out what was wrong with them. The major-ity were very old, almost ancient you could say. For example, most photocopiers now are digital, but these were analogue and ten, maybe fifteen years obsolete in the UK. We had a vast array of different styles of photocopiers to work on, all in different states of repair. To take one example, the garrison clerks would keep their photocopier immaculate, even though they'd used it ten thousand times more than, say, the artillery's photocopier, which was a battered piece of equipment because every gunnery sergeant major that came in would slam his piece of paper down, smash his hand on the cover and rip the paper out of it at the end. The garrison admin office knew that if they mistreated their copier it would fail them and then they would be without a valued piece of equipment, whereas if the gunnery sergeant major broke his photocopier, he'd just get two of his gunners to sit down and write whatever he wanted copying.

The most memorable photocopier job was flying out to Mount Byron, which is a separate island. We were replacing a machine that wasn't big enough to do the job with one that is totally digital and as close to up to date as you could get.

We had to get on a helicopter with this huge photocopier and after we were dropped off at the landing point in Byron, we put the copier into a tracked vehicle, which trundled up a two-mile stretch of rocky, bumpy, mountain track. Photocopiers are sensitive bits of kit, but we got it up to the base in one piece, unpackaged it and spent the next forty-eight hours bringing it back to life after its rather drastic travel arrangements. Actually, when we told Ricoh how we got it there, they were quite impressed that their machine could survive the rigours of what we'd put it through.

I liked the Falklands immensely. I would quite happily go

there again. Some of the scenery is breathtaking. I took hundreds of photos out there. I've got a photo of a dolphin: even though it's just a speck in the water, *I* know it's a dolphin. And plenty of cheeky-looking penguins – I could enter some of those for prizes. I have pictures of Spud too, although I doubt I could enter them for anything other than the 'embarrassing photos' category.

COMBAT SUPPORT ARMS

The Combat Support Arms provide direct support to the Combat Arms and include artillery, engineer, signals and intelligence.

Royal Regiment of Artillery
Corps of Royal Engineers
Royal Corps of Signals
Intelligence Corps

CAPTAIN IMRAN AHMED

'Everyone in the Engineers wants to blow up a bridge...'

I was the troop commander for a close support troop of Royal Engineers. My squadron was held back from Operation Telic to support 3 Commando Brigade on Operation Herrick 9 in Afghanistan. Close support is officially for 'support, survivability and sustainability' – basically, letting the field army survive and fight on the ground. It also includes building and improving forward operating bases, which we ended up doing in Garmsir.

When we first got there, the guys were living in huts, which leaked quite considerably, and there were mice running around the floor. It was not very nice at all. By the time we had finished, they were living in big canvas tents with electricity. Every tent had lights and at least one plug socket so they could recharge something. Some even had heating – it was far more comfortable than before. As time went on, we ended up building quite a few new bits and pieces, more accommodation and briefing areas, and generally making the conditions more comfortable for the guys living there. They were most impressed by the work we did.

We also provided mobility support, which in Afghanistan meant looking for IEDs on major routes when requested to do so. My lads would double up as infantry soldiers to help relieve the pressure on their troops, who were very thin on the ground at times.

We were also called in for explosive support. For example, if the infantry came across a compound they wanted to use as a good piece of cover, we would be there with explosives ready to blow a hole in the wall so they could get in. My lads carry half bar mines, which are handy four-kilo lumps of explosive originally designed to blow up Russian tanks in the Cold War. Take one of those, add a detonator, some fuse cord and push the plunger, which sets off the fuse, and it's like your fizzing time bomb in a Tom and Jerry cartoon – maybe slightly more sophisticated.

We didn't get to blow anything up, so I didn't get the chance to use them, which was a pity – everyone in the Engineers wants to blow up a bridge because we do a lot of bridge demolition work in our counter-mobility training, stopping the enemy from crossing that river. Actually, I've never blown up a bridge, although we have built a few in Afghanistan.

The first couple of patrols with the infantry were scary. I definitely remember being quite nervous for the first few minutes after walking out of the patrol base. This was the first time I had gone out specifically to look for a fight. Actually, I don't think I had got into a fight before that since secondary school. Every step you take you don't know what could happen, whether you might step on something or whether you're walking into an ambush. You are hyper-aware, looking around all the time, and very focused on everything going on around you.

We did a couple of compound clearances and on those occasions the adrenalin rises because you're running into this compound, you don't know if there are people in there or what's going to happen. Nothing happened. And we didn't get attacked either – we didn't even see the enemy on that particular patrol. To be honest, I felt a bit disappointed coming back after this whole long patrol having had no contact. At the same time, you can't help but feel happy that the blokes you were with didn't get into danger that day.

The next patrol, the infantry OC thought it would be a brilliant idea to drop down into the river basin and follow the river before coming back into the Green Zone to assault a couple of villages. His plan was that we would disappear and then reappear, and the Taliban would think, Oooh, where have they come from? We'd take them by surprise. We ended up walking through some horrible, stagnating, swampy grasslands to get down to this place and the point where we popped up was right on the edge of a village. A couple of kids, dressed in really bright colours, were sitting and playing on a log outside a hut. Behind the house, they had just pulled out the corn harvest – you had the husks and stalks of the harvest, the muted brown of the buildings while the sky was this extraordinarily brilliant blue: if I had been able to get my camera out, it would have probably been a great photograph, but as we were just about to start an assault, it wasn't appropriate or sensible to do so. Yet again, though, there was no enemy contact.

I am quite a keen photographer and my memories of Afghanistan are now all tied up with my best photographs. Filling Hesco at sunset, with the clouds of dust making a horrifically dusty environment is one shot. My favourite photo is FOB Delhi right at the beginning of the tour. Flying into or out of a place by helicopter is always exciting, and a Chinook had just flown in and the Princess of Wales's Regiment was getting ready to leave. I got a brilliant photograph of all their blokes in a straight line, waiting to get on to the helicopter. Even though you can't directly tell these guys are going home, you get a sense that it is an ending.

Two weeks before I was due to leave theatre and return home, we were on another fighting patrol, looking for the Taliban. I still hadn't seen any Taliban, although I had seen some dickers, the guys that ride around on the motorbikes watching what we are doing, and I had found an IED earlier in the tour. We had been rocketed a couple of times, so there was stuff going on.

I was out with some of my sappers, providing explosive support for 5 Platoon, ready to blow up anything they wanted us to blow up. We were supposed to go about ten kilometres south, break into a compound, sleep in the compound, and do some patrols overnight from there, looking for stuff we could blow up.

Six hours into the patrol we came under contact from a sniper. For about an hour and a half, he was firing single shots at us. He fired about six or seven times and each time we would return fire and then move forward to try and identify where he was going. If it had been heavy and sustained contact, like some of my colleagues had been involved in, that might have made more sense, but this was so silly, literally one bloke firing single shots.

Nevertheless, some of the shots were quite close and it was a sur-real feeling to be shot at.

At one point we were all stood along this tree-lined road. He must have had a pretty good view of us and suddenly five shots rang out, and one of them went through my knee. It didn't hurt much straight away. It was more like being kicked in a play-ground argument, but when I looked down, my leg was bleeding a little bit and it finally dawned on me: 'Oh my gosh, I've been shot.' I scrambled from where I was and jumped into a ditch full of muddy water right next to me – which in hindsight I should have been in before for cover – while everyone else returned fire at this guy, and waited for the medic to come along.

The medic was in the patrol, so within twenty-five metres of where I was, but I also had Sapper James Mooney right next to me and he had first-aid training. He started putting a dressing on my leg and tried to sort it out. But then the sergeant shouted that we were in danger where we were and told us to get to him, so we climbed over a wall to get into the compound. In my mind I ran perfectly fine, but it's quite possible that James helped me.

The infantry guys formed a perimeter and kept returning fire, and finally drove this sniper off and secured the area, and I got CASEVACed by helicopter straight to hospital in Camp Bastion. I was there within an hour, and two hours later I was on the phone to my mum. I told her I had got shot and tried to reassure her I was going to be fine – although at that point it wasn't guar-anteed. Apparently the bullet had passed very close to the artery at the back of my knee. If it had been any closer I could have ended up having my leg amputated. I hadn't quite realised the severity of it. Within twenty-four hours you have your trauma risk-management meeting, which is a process designed to identify the onset of PTSD. Basically, someone comes along to talk to you about what has happened. But even from the moment it happened, I was laughing and joking about being shot and very relaxed about it, and to be honest that's never changed. Yes, it was a close shave, and it could have been a lot worse, but it wasn't.

They kept me in Bastion for four days and then flew me back to Selly Oak, which was a brilliant, excellent hospital. I was really looked after well. My parents came to see me. They live in Birmingham anyway, so they were close. They are both nurses – my dad is a psychiatric nurse and my mum is a maternity nurse – so they understand about infection and all those lovely things. It was quite a shocking experience for them seeing me like that, but they have dealt with it reasonably well. It is less than six months since it happened and I am still in rehab for my leg, but I think it's about 80 to 90 per cent of the way there, which is not too bad.

CAPTAIN MAX CHENERY

'Bliffed black riding boots...'

I was out in Iraq and Afghanistan, but there is a lot of variety within the Artillery, so I knew I could swap between the different parts. I have ridden horses all my life and the opportunity to go to the King's Troop and do the ceremonial mounted stuff was definitely something I wanted to do.

The King's Troop is the Queen's ceremonial saluting battery. It was formed in 1946 by the then king, George VI, the Queen's father, who decided he wanted to keep a saluting battery for royal salutes and the like. Originally, they were called the Riding Troop, but when the King visited them in October 1947, he was so impressed, he changed their name to the King's Troop and that stuck, and the Queen has kept that name too.

Like any unit of the Household Troops, our role as display troops is to be in the public eye. We do the big salutes in London for the Queen's birthday, accession to the throne and that kind of stuff, the state opening of Parliament, salutes for the Duke of Edinburgh's birthday, the Queen's coronation. We also do musical drives, from the Horse of the Year Show at Olympia through to some agricultural shows in the summer period.

All our horses are grouped into colours. There are six sub-sections, running from A to F, A being the lightest bay horses. They get darker and darker until F, which is the black horses. If there are any big state funerals, the King's Troop will be involved with our black horses.

The officers' chargers are all over 17 hands. They are bigger than the soldiers' horses, which are 15.2 to 16.2 hands. I have two horses, William and Tom, and they're both from the Continent. Of course, with that goes certain characteristics, so fairly stubborn, which is often the way with warmblood horses. Actually, Tom isn't at all suitable – he is terrified of everything really, and pretty bad in heavy traffic, which isn't ideal for central London. A lot of people don't like William because he sometimes just stops and refuses to do anything, although I'm getting along quite well with him at the moment. But we'll see if he improves. I have yet to ride in any big parades with him.

I've only been in the job for six months, but I have done a salute in Green Park and Hyde Park – basically, gallop on, fire the guns and then gallop off – also a military tattoo at the Royal Windsor Horse Show, where we perform our musical drive, and the West Midlands Show, in Shropshire, with all six gun teams.

The gun teams use thirteen-pounder guns that were made in 1904. All of them were fired in the First and Second World Wars. In the First World War the guns fired as conventional artillery and in the Second World War they were used for air defence. I don't know quite how successful they were in the Second World War in the air defence role – you've got to be very lucky to hit a plane firing an artillery piece with one of those, especially a thirteen-pounder, which has a maximum range of just 6700 yards. Only one gun can still fire live rounds and that will be used for accompanying the Queen's coffin at her funeral. The others now only fire blank rounds.

Our ceremonial uniform's not too bad to ride in – it's not like the Household Cavalry, with their metal breastplates and metal hats. We wear bliffed black riding boots, spurs, a set of dark-blue britches with a red stripe down the side, and a fairly tight-fitting blue jacket with gold braid across the front and gold epaulettes. We also wear a gold crossbelt, a set of lines, which is a gold piece of rope that hangs around the chest, and a busby hat with a long white plume. On the side of the hat, there is what we call a 'busby bag', which is a big strip of red cloth that was originally filled with wet sand to stop the sword blade hitting you.

We need our soldiers to be first-rate horsemen to perform the demanding and potentially dangerous musical drives: our soldiers have to be able to control groups of horses pulling the large gun carriages at speed.

That is very different from the Household Cavalry soldiers, who perform a slower role. They trot their horses from Knightsbridge to Buckingham Palace daily – as you can tell, there is great friendly rivalry and banter between them and us. To be honest, the Household Cavalry do quite a different job. Obviously they do Guards' work mostly, so their job is a lot slower, everything is slower paced. They do their stuff at Horse Guards Parade and they're very good at looking smart. Our job is slightly faster paced, which probably requires a better standard of jockeying. I think they would admit that.

CORPORAL CRAIG JOHNSON*

'That's why we're called pongos . . .'

I'm part of the Army's surveillance and target acquisition patrols. We put observation posts into high-risk areas, quite close to where the enemy force is, and try to identify targets of interest.

A couple of weeks before any op, we move into a secure covert location to see how the civilians live their life. Once we have gained a good idea of how they go through their daily activities, we can start looking for discrepancies, like people in that area who shouldn't be there. If we are in a community where there are mainly women looking after kids and a lot of young men arrive, you'll start thinking, Hey, there's something wrong here. Also, people digging in areas that are not obviously meant to be dug automatically flags up something we can look at.

On some operations we have to go sub-surface, which is digging a hide underground and camouflaging it. We sometimes live there for two or three weeks. We'll make a hide about two metres by two metres, a metre deep, and lay a support structure out of branches, placing swards of grass over to camouflage it. The big problem then is we have extracted a lot of soil, so it's a case of putting it in our bergens and finding an area to dump it that's not going to be obvious. An ideal place would be a river-bank where there have been collapses. If we dump our soil there, it just looks like a continuation of the collapse.

Our field craft has to be quite a high standard as we have to move from one environment to another without leaving any signs behind for the enemy to see and give us away. Don't step on a log because you will leave markings on the dead bark. Brushing against leaves will turn them out at a slightly different angle from their surrounding leaves, which will stand out to your trackers, as will broken twigs and flattened grass. The biggest one is transfer-ence – the movement of mud from your boots, which is going to leave imprints.

It is all about picking your route and checking your back route, i.e. where you have just been, all the time. When you are moving along as a group, the last man's job is to stop every now and again and have a look behind him. If he notices the grass has been trampled down, then he has to tease it out with his hand and bring it back up. And one final important thing essential for camouflage: we stop washing weeks before we go into the field. That's why we're called pongos. We do get dirty and I suppose a bit smelly, but soap, shampoo or deodorant give out scent waves from a long distance away. They're really, really obvious.

I've been lucky to have been on a number of operational tours to Afghanistan. It was coming into winter on my first tour, some of the most brutal weather I have ever experienced; a mixture of heavy snow and rain, which turned the desert to a dirty-brown-coloured slurry. Even the tracked vehicles were bogging in under the conditions. So it was a case of having a Napoleonic winter – all soldiering stopped while everyone waited for the summer season when we could carry on.

But the most recent tour was the absolute pinnacle of my career so far. The snow had cleared away this time, but it was very, very cold. In fact, the interpreters were telling us it was the coldest winter for a great many years.

This op wasn't sub-surface, just the opposite. We climbed up into the mountains, camouflaged ourselves among the rocks and lived there for about three weeks. Nine times out of ten we pongos patrol in by foot, so we have to carry everything in our bergens – all our ammunition, communications, rations and water. So you are carrying a lot.

There was just the six of us, good friends who had learned to work together. I couldn't have asked for a better patrol to be honest with you. We had to have hard routine on this op, where you urinate in bottles, defecate into bags and keep them with you until you return. And no fires can be lit. They would stand out a mile away. Rations had to be eaten cold, which is fine by me because I like my rations cold, although the other guys were not so happy about that.

You are always busy on these ops. There are always two guys on, one's observing and the other's a sentry. The two who have come off have to do the administration, clean the weapons, check the radio/communication equipment – only after this can they catch up on any sleep.

We report every bit of information we see to our troop

commander and it's up to him, or the troop sergeant major (TSM), to pick out the relevant aspects. We also take a lot of photographs and send the imagery back to brigade headquarters for them to analyse and pick out any specific targets. If they are after a particular person, we can photograph a range of individuals. After these are analysed, they can decide, 'OK, that's the guy we are after,' and organise a mission.

Watching a community coming alive in a remote part of Afghanistan is fascinating. We are talking about a lifestyle two or three hundred years behind us – imagine scenes straight out of the Bible, that sort of thing. Just before the sun comes up, the womenfolk light the fires to start the cooking. The smoke comes curling up from the different compounds. Then the farmers go out to start the day's work and a little while later the kids go out with the goats and sheep, and the nomads cross the desert with trains of camels – and six guys from Britain are sat up a mountain top watching all this in secret. It is fantastic.

Eventually the day winds down. The wives start up the fires again to cook the evening meals, the kids come back home shortly after that with the goats, and the farmers work until they cannot see the hand in front of their face. That marks the end of the day for civilians, but that is when it can get interesting for us.

We use our thermal imagery and night vision. The detail isn't 100 per cent, but you can tell the difference between guys with weapons and farmers with tools. We saw a lot of activity this time: armed men digging on roads and we reported that back. We watched bikers going up and down the wadi all night, resupplying and moving men or soldiers into an area to question the locals to find out if they have seen British troops. These civilians find themselves in very difficult circumstances. All they are trying to do is lead their lives, so they will tell the Taliban or other insurgents what they want to hear, not because they want to inflict violence upon us, but to keep their families safe. It's nothing personal.

WARRANT OFFICER CLASS 2 TOM SAUNDERS*
'Sensory overload . . .'

I remember watching television as a very young boy and there was an advert with a bloke and his girlfriend in a sports car on a nice summer's day. He looks in his rearview mirror and a troop of Scimitar tanks overtake him, and I just thought, Wow, how cool. I joined the Territorial Army while I was still at school, and then my local cavalry regiment.

My first operation was Cyprus, when we were driving Ferret Scout cars, tiny four-wheel-drive armoured cars. We patrolled the borders between the Turks and the Greeks, and were supposed to stop them from fighting, although we didn't actually see any fighting there.

Bosnia kicked off in 1991, and I was a commander of a Scimitar. A Scimitar is a light tank – it weighs ten tons and is made out of aluminium to keep the weight down. In effect it has the same amount of armour as a coke can, but it's fast, very fast, and that is what you use to your advantage.

Driving a tracked vehicle is like being in a boat: you sway

about and how comfortable you are depends on how good your driver is. It's noisy, smelly, dirty and cramped, especially in all your body armour. It can be way too hot in summer and freezing cold in winter – when it's really cold, your skin sticks to the metal, so you've got to wear contact gloves. But you become quite attached to it. It gives you protection, it's got your cooking equipment in it, it becomes your little home from home. Every vehicle has its own personality. Some people have names for their vehicles, but I used to call ours all sorts of things, depending on what it was doing. If it broke down, obviously I can't tell you what I called it, but I used to pat it like a horse if it got us out of trouble. If you got moved off your vehicle, the replacement was never quite the same and you were always keen to get back to yours. Probably the best thing about mine was how tough it was. In winter conditions, we rolled it three times in a week in the mountains, but after a minor bit of fettling by the crew it still worked. You could always get the thing going, that was the beauty of it. The worst thing was the steering, that wasn't up to much, and in winter it was a cow to move. If you stayed still for any period of time, you'd freeze to the floor, so you'd have to get the crowbars out and unfreeze yourself from the ground. Also, she used to conk out every now and again because water would get through the fuel lines and freeze. You would have to put your lighter on the petrol pipe to defrost the water that had frozen the pipes, which is never a good thing to do.

There were three of us in the tank. I was twenty-four, so I thought I was quite old then, and I had two seventeen-year-old boys under my command, Trooper Oliver and Trooper Tansey. They were typical seventeen-year-olds. I mean, they talked about football boots and trainers, and I'd sit there and think, Oh God! But we were comfortable with each other and it was easy to work together. Tansey, the driver, was straight out of school. He used to pull faces behind my back, but I would always catch him out. He was rubbish at maintaining the vehicle, but he could drive it and that's what I needed. Oliver, who had bum fluff on his top lip, couldn't fight his way out of a paper bag. But he could shoot – he was a bloody good gunner and that's what you wanted. They were good boys, really.

We were there to protect UN convoys. United Nations Protection Force, they called us. Humanitarian convoys were going between all the warring factions, but the convoys were open to attack by whichever side the aid wasn't going to. We were there to keep the routes open and make sure the convoys got through. We'd picket the routes: we would be at the major junctions and choke points, and react if there was any trouble.

This was the first time I came under mortar artillery fire and got shot at. The first occasion I was in the turret of my vehicle and machine-gun fire started coming down, and I felt huge. I thought everybody was shooting at me specifically. I didn't feel panic so much as I couldn't believe what was happening: I'm being shot at here!

I saw dead bodies for the first time too. On picket duty early one morning, an open truck went by, just stacked up to the top with bodies, which was shocking. You couldn't believe what you were seeing because you'd never seen it before. It's like, 'Did I just see a load of dead bodies stacked up in the back of that truck?' A lot of times we would see people shooting each other up. Waves of people being mowed down. It was so casual, that was the worst thing. It's a major assault on your senses, like sensory overload. But you sort of get used to it and then it becomes normal.

It was my first insight into what war was all about and I just thought, What an absolute and utter waste. I don't really understand the politics behind it, but as far as I could see, neighbours, who had lived together for hundreds of years, turned on each other, just like that. I asked a Bosnian once where his family were. 'They're in the garden.' 'What do you mean, "They're in the garden"?' It turns out they were buried in the garden. His neighbours had killed them because he was a Bosnian Muslim and the neighbours were Serbs, and all of a sudden they'd become deadly enemies. We humans call ourselves civilised, but at a moment's notice that thin veneer is dropped and we become animals.

I tried to explain things to my dad when I was on R & R. 'Dad, you know when you walk down the street in England, you expect to get to the other end, knowing nothing's going to happen? Well, when you go to a war zone all of that is taken away, all the rules are gone, and you walk out and think, Right, I could die at any moment and nobody, including the police, are going to come and help me.'

After four tours of Bosnia, I went to Iraq, and it was relatively quiet for us. We only had one bloke shot. That was just absolutely fantastic fun. We had guns, bombs, grenades, plenty of fuel, plenty of water.

We did desert patrols. My particular troop had WMIKs, which look like Land Rovers with cut-down bodywork. They've got no windscreen and are configured for desert patrols. They are designed to be fast and to scoot about the desert, so have an upgraded suspension – they're very cool.

It was our job to train the Iraqis, but after a very short time, we realised they weren't really listening. We went after bandit groups who would hijack cars off the motorway, steal equipment and shoot the drivers. If they hopped on their vehicles, you'd have a chase through the desert for the rest of the day. We would never catch them, basically because they had faster vehicles than us. The WMIKs can go eighty miles an hour, but these guys had Land Cruisers, which just fly – plus, obviously, they knew the area.

But a lot of it was good fun. Going on patrol is fun. You're scared. It's like, what's going to happen? Am I going to run over a mine? You get shot at, mortared, things like that. Friends from my troop were blown up with a mine, but luckily they were injured and not killed. When it's all finished and over, you smile and giggle with each other like little kids. It's a release, a buzz. You have to push yourself forward sometimes because you don't want to go forward, but you do, and you realise at the end of the day, I can hack it. A lot of soldiering is proving to yourself you can do it, and it's quite addictive.

BOMBARDIER ZOË SAVAGE

'Punch, punch, punch . . .'

I deployed to Bosnia when I was eighteen, which was quite daunting to start with. For one thing, I'd never been abroad before; that was my first time on a plane. I was only a gunner at the time, so I would do cordons where I had to stop people coming into an area – although as an eighteen-year-old female I probably didn't look very fierce. They must have looked at me and thought, She's not up to much.

After that I went to Iraq on Telic 2. We used to help the infantry doing search operations. When we went into a village, the men would get detained and I would have to search all the females and children. The women were really frightened and they'd be shouting and screaming and asking where their husbands were.

Nevertheless, we had a honeymoon period for a short time after the war had finished – they thought we were the best thing since sliced bread then. But a couple of months into our tour, certain parts of the city would turn on us. Basra was always the place you had to be the most vigilant. It was a very agitated town. The whole place stank. There was rubbish and flies everywhere. There was no care or vigilance on the road. They would drive a hundred miles an hour in these lethal cars that looked like bangers.

I remember one day turning into this street in our Land Rover and hundreds of people just closed in on us and started throwing stones. I was driving and my boss, who was next to me, said, 'We need to get out of here – put your foot down.' I didn't panic. I just focused on getting out and drove through it, at speed, with stones smashing against the windows. My heart was going extra fast. These things do test you, but I'm glad it happened because I coped with it really well, and I now know I can cope under pressure.

In May this year, we held the first Gunner Boxing Competition, which is a big deal in the Artillery. I had dabbled a little bit in boxing before, sparring with the lads. But I'd never got to fight because there was nobody within my weight category to fight against, even though I was eighty kilograms at that time as I'd just had my eldest daughter and was struggling to lose the baby weight.

But this time, when our battery quartermaster sergeant (BQMS) got a team together, there were a few female gunners fighting at my weight level, so I could enter the competition. I found out I was fighting Sarah Sanderson from 32 Regiment, who is a lance-bombardier. Everyone kept coming up to me and saying, 'Zoë, have you seen her? She looks massive!' I also heard she was quite strong. Apparently she did lots of weights in the gym and she'd been punching blokes and they'd been really stunned by her power. I was apprehensive about it. Actually, I was dead nervous.

The night itself was unbelievable. About eight hundred people were watching. Lance-Bombardier Sanderson went out first and I thought she looked very strong. I'm five-nine and she's a little shorter, although a lot stockier than me. You have your own song to go out to and hers was supposed to be 'In for the Kill' by La Roux, but they didn't have it, which I thought was quite good for me, as that must have unsettled her. Fortunately, they had my song, 'She's a Rebel', by Green Day. I came out of the tent when that started playing. Everyone was cheering and the adrenalin was pumping. When the bell rang, my coach said, 'Just go in there and do your best, I know you can win.'

If I'm honest, she was all over me in that first round. She came in close and punched me a good few times. I could feel the power of her punches and my head went back and I stumbled a little bit. But I could take it, the punches weren't hurting, which is weird. I just kept repeating in my mind, I'm going to beat you, my husband's out there watching, I've got two kids, I'm going to beat you. And then it was toe to toe, punch for punch, all the way, but she definitely got the better of me the first round.

I went back to my corner and as I sat down, my coach went, 'I can tell you now, you've got a black eye, but don't worry about that.' I didn't feel any pain and I was raring to go. My coach sprayed me with water and told me to keep my guard up.

For the first thirty seconds of the second round, she punched me quite a few times, but then she tired out. That's when I went in. Punch, punch, punch, and all my punches were scoring blows. We got a standing ovation after that second round, which was just the best feeling in the world. I've never felt so exhilarated in my life. It was brilliant, fantastic.

Just before the third round, my coach said, 'Try and do something different because she knows what you're going to do.' I tried body shots and different combinations, and really began to knock her about.

At the end, the referee held our wrists, ready to put up the hand of the winner, and then came the announcement. 'By unanimous decision . . . blue is the winner,' which was me.

As soon as I got into the changing room, I couldn't stop crying with all that adrenalin, and the fact that I had won and hadn't been hurt or injured. I've spoken with Sarah a few times since and she said she was very emotional after the fight too.

We went to the sergeants' mess afterwards for a curry and a drink, and everyone said it was the best fight of the night. The commanding officer, Lieutenant Colonel Thornhill, came into the mess and bought two bottles of champagne for us, which we were drinking out of the trophy.

My regiment (40th Royal Artillery) is in Afghanistan at the moment, but I couldn't go because I am teaching Royal Artillery Trade Training to Phase 2 recruits. We've lost two people from the regiment. One of them I knew really well, Bombardier Craig Hopson. He was in a vehicle with the infantry and it went over an IED. Craig was lovely: a big, broad Yorkshire lad, rugby player, brash, fun, always laughing and joking with people. He would brighten up a room when he walked in. I cried when I heard he'd died because he was just twenty-four years old and he'd got a baby girl. You expect it to happen in our job, but when it does happen, you're shocked. I went to Wootton Bassett for the repatriation and the streets of the town were full of people, which was fantastic. I think it is amazing what those people do. They even close their shops, which they don't have to do, but it shows the appreciation they have for us. That is so nice because sometimes you don't feel appreciated by civilians.

I really want to go to Afghanistan. I want to prove to people that you can have a family and still be operationally deployable, because some people, maybe older people, think females shouldn't be in the Army, and certainly don't think you should have children and be in the Army. I might be a couple of years behind career path-wise because I've had to take time out to give birth, and with six months' maternity leave, it does put you back. But my regiment were very good. They put me on leadership courses as soon as I came back and then promoted me. So they must think I have something, which obviously makes me feel very proud.

COMBAT ARMS

The Combat Arms are the 'teeth' of the British Army – infantry, armoured and aviation units that engage in close action.

Royal Armoured Corps
Infantry
Special Forces
Army Air Corps

CAPTAIN SAM AIKEN

'Everyone always asks what it's like to be shot...'

I have always wanted to be a soldier, which is an odd one family-wise, as my parents and my brother are all artists. I'm a bit of a black sheep in that way. I knew I wanted to go into the infantry. I didn't originally have the Paras down, but my sergeant major at Sandhurst was a paratrooper and he basically came up to me one day and said, '*You* are going on a visit to 1 PARA.' All the soldiers there loved the job, couldn't wait to go on their next tour, and I just thought, Perfect, that's exactly what I want to be a part of.

My first operation was Herrick 8 with 2 PARA. We were Battle Group North in Helmand. My company group went out to FOB Gibraltar, which is a forward operating base in the Upper Gereshk Valley. We provided a breakwater between Gereshk and Sangin. Our role was to prevent Taliban insurgence between the two towns, to stop them having dominance over the Green Zone in that area and to provide reassurance to the local population as to the legitimacy of the Islamic government of Afghanistan and ISAF.

I absolutely loved being out there. It was great to go off and do real, actual soldiering. Finally, you're putting into practice everything you've learned, and it was fantastic, really good fun. Literally the best times of my life were out there, but also some of the most horrific experiences and some of the saddest times as well.

We were the advance party for the main body of 2 PARA, one of the first flights out to theatre, and we went straight forward to FOB Gibraltar. My second day in Afghanistan, I went on a familiarisation patrol with the Marines, who we were replacing, and came under contact with the Taliban about five hundred metres outside the base. We got ambushed.

By later standards it was quite a low-scale fight, but at the time it seemed pretty hectic. Five or six Taliban hit us with small arms and RPG, and one of the Marines had his Camelbak shot straight through and got splinters in his arms. In all fairness to the Marine platoon commander, he did a really good job – rapidly pushed the enemy off their position and chased them away. The platoon killed one Taliban and shot another one's hand off. But I don't know how on Earth no one else got hurt because they were so close when they initiated the contact.

That was a good blooding. I got back from that TIC and thought, Fantastic. Everyone had a good buzz. We'd routed the enemy and got back nice and safely. I found it amazing that the drills we'd been taught in training really did kick in as second nature. Little things, like RTR, for example, return fire, take cover, return accurate fire. We saw where the enemy were, fired in a vague direction, got into some good cover and then started returning accurate fire from that position. Several times I found myself thinking, What do I need to do next? and I'd already done it.

But, bloody hell, it was hard work. Absolutely shattering. The heat is exhausting in Afghanistan. It's so oppressive. You're constantly sweating and it saps your strength and energy. I remember thinking the Marines must feel we're incredibly unfit because all of our blokes were exhausted. We expected heat, but you can't train for it in England, you can't prepare yourself for the fact that you're running around with eighty pounds of kit in a sauna. I mean, one day we clocked a temperature of fifty-seven degrees. That initial couple of weeks was really hard work. We had to compensate for it and limit our patrols to shorter distances, and go out at dusk and dawn when it was cooler. After about four weeks, your body finally acclimatises.

We also used to go out on these mobile patrols in Viking armoured vehicles, out into the desert and laager up for the night, before punching into the Green Zone at dawn the next day. I'm probably sounding a bit lame now, but the desert was beautiful, with more stars in the night skies than you've ever seen. If you had a five-star hotel where our FOB was, you could charge thousands of pounds a night. The view was gorgeous, poppy fields for two hundred metres, followed by desert, followed by big snow-capped mountains under a really blue sky. Lovely country – shame about the people, though.

Actually, because the Taliban were doing their opium harvest at that time, we had two months where it was quite quiet, just a few small incidents – a couple of IED strikes on our armoured vehicles, little things like that. I think the Taliban were using it as as much of a training period as us, to be honest.

I went away on R & R back to England. I had just landed into Brize Norton when one of the RAF officers asked for me over the speaker and told me I needed to phone my battalion. He'd heard there had been an incident with 8 Platoon and there were casualties.

I phoned the guardroom and got a guard commander from 2 PARA: 'Can you tell me exactly what's happened?'

'Yes, sir,' he said. 'Lance Corporal James Bateman and Private Doherty were killed in an ambush yesterday morning.'

'You've got to have that wrong,' I said. 'It must be wrong.' Just hoping against hope.

That was hideous. A couple of blokes who I had been looking after for nearly a year – leading, living with day in, day out – ever since taking command of my platoon in England, and to realise that both of them had been killed as soon as I had left them was absolutely awful. I just felt really helpless and tried to get straight back, but they wouldn't let me.

People always say the best soldiers are the ones to die first, which sounds like a cliché, but those two were the real characters of the platoon. People you really warmed to. When things were hard, they would be able to say something that would take your mind off your problems or make you laugh. Private Doherty was full of life, bloody good at his job, and loved being in the Reg. He used to have a T-shirt, 'Private Doherty . . . I Hate Hats!' The Parachute Regiment refers to everyone else in the Army as a 'hat', but he quite adamantly disliked them all. It was shocking he was killed – and two days after his twentieth birthday as well.

Corporal Bateman, again, great character, a big, friendly giant. He was one of those people who would do anything to help someone, a really solid, dependable guy. It was such a shock to think he wasn't going to be there when I got back.

So that put quite a dampener on the R & R, as you can imagine. I was going to take my girlfriend away – the original plan had been Egypt, but I said no way on earth did I want to go anywhere with sun and sand. In the end we didn't go anywhere, as I was asked to speak at both of the funerals, in different parts of the country, and of course I wanted to attend. I needed time to work out what I'd say, as this was my first time talking to relatives.

Five men from our battalion had been killed and they were all coming home together; the battalion organised for all the families to stay in a hotel the night before the repatriation service at Lyneham. I went down and met with Lance Corporal Bateman's and Private Doherty's families. Both families hadn't seen them for four months, and I had seen both of them just two days before, so I printed off everything I had on my camera of those two, and I hoped that was something they were happy to receive.

I had never been to a repatriation before. I stood behind the families, along with some of the other military staff, and I felt a bit of an intruder really because there were grieving mothers and family crying in front of me, sitting on rows of chairs in a marquee facing out into the airfield. The plane taxis in and then the coffins come off one by one with a bearer party, which then marches each from the plane into the hearse. To be honest, that felt rather unreal for me. I couldn't relate the coffins to the blokes I'd been on patrol with a few days before. The coffins were then taken in a funeral procession through the local town, Wootton Bassett, along streets lined with people paying their respects.

After I'd gone to the two funerals, it was the end of my leave. I flew back to Afghanistan – straight into a bit of a hornets' nest, basically. The harvest season was over, and what I suppose you could describe as the Taliban's summer offensive had begun.

When I landed in the FOB, my platoon sergeant said, 'We're about to go on patrol in half an hour, sir. Do you want to come or do you want to get yourself sorted?' I said, 'No, I'll come out on this as well.' Got a quick brief on where we were going, what we were doing, took over the command, and out we went – and walked into an ambush about two hundred metres down the road, a big ambush, actually. You know, a proper fight. Welcome back to Afghanistan, Sam.

We pinned them with mortars, fixed them in position, and put on a right flanking attack and cleared it out. We cleared about fifteen compounds and undoubtedly killed a good few that day – we saw a lot of blood trails, flip-flops covered in blood, things like that, which was good. In fact, it felt awesome to hit back, especially as they had ambushed us and we had turned it on them.

Suddenly every patrol turned into a fight. Instead of walking miles to get into an area where we thought the flak was, we were being hit right outside our front door. My platoon went out the next day, twenty-four-strong. We got the first eight men out of the gate – and came under contact. We had to fight our way out and across the bridges over the canal into the compounds nearby. That was another good day, fantastic. We called in some air power and artillery and mortar, and I got to use all the weapons

106

in my arsenal as a platoon commander, and to really ply my trade, which was great fun. Just one of my men, a TA reservist, was wounded. A piece of RPG went through his leg, but it was just a flesh wound. It was kind of funny. There is a video of him being treated in the med room, and people are taking the piss out of him for getting in the way. 'TA, that's why you got hit. You're too fat, too slow. You should have better drills.' But thankfully he healed up completely and went back to his job in London.

A couple of days after that, we went out on a clearance patrol. I had planned a patrol of one of the areas to dominate the ground and reassure the locals we were still out and about, but a second objective was to push out nice and quiet, and sneak into the back of this vineyard, maybe catch some Taliban there. We had established a couple of areas we thought were the enemy's forming-up points – the places where they'd collect before moving off to do attacks. We had taken fire from this particular vineyard during the last contact.

We moved a really roundabout route and it obviously worked because they hadn't picked us up. Normally it's the other way around: they're firing first on us. We moved up near to the vineyard, stopped, and the snipers began scanning a bit of open ground. One of them said, 'Boss, there's five or six blokes with weapons in that tree line opposite us.' I had a good look at them and they had two machine guns, AK47s, plus a couple of guys with RPGs.

I ordered two sections lined up in a base line and asked the fire support team to get co-ordinates ready for the mortars and guns. I had my platoon sergeant and another section out at the back to make sure we were secure, and told the air controller to alert any air around that we were probably going to be in a TIC soon. I had the snipers next to me, so after we had positively identified them as enemy, we would guarantee at least one killed before they could take cover. I also had the whole platoon on orders on the radio: 'As soon as the sniper fires, everyone else is to fire at the Taliban locations previously indicated.' We were watching this one fellow patrol down the tree line and I said, 'Yeah, OK, Corporal, fire.' That was the first time I had ever directly ordered someone killed.

Bang. Looking through my scope, I watched the guy fall and then everyone else on both sides of me started firing. The tree line just erupted and I am pretty sure we killed all five of them. You could see them on the floor. I decided to go left-flanking. I left a fire base there and took two sections to flank round another ditch and get up on to that position, so we could collect the weapons, check they were dead and get any intelligence that was there. Then that would be it, job done.

I was just behind the lead section, in quite close undergrowth, when two other Taliban ran out in front of us, about a hundred metres from where we had been firing. The lead scout and the commander of the assaulting section shot them and they fell down in the rubble of this old bombed building. But we then got fired on from another compound a hundred metres away off to our left. I asked the forward air controller next to me to get some air. He called in an Apache, which had already fired on that first position for us, and gave a grid reference, a direction of bearing from the previous strike and a compound number for where the enemy were. He asked them to fire.

Well, for some unknown reason, the Apache pilot fired into our tree line instead of theirs, three bursts of twenty rounds of high-explosive shells.

Maybe it's just standard operating procedures, but the American pilots come down nice and low when they are preparing to attack someone so they can see what's happening. Then they fire. Our pilots stay very high, out of range of anything the enemy can fire back, although I've been told that their weapons systems and target-acquisition bits are better than the Americans'. I just don't know.

When an attack helicopter is firing at someone else, it makes a rhythmic dull thud. When it's directed at you, it's magnified hugely; the sound was much louder than I'd ever heard before. When the first round came through the trees, the branches were breaking directly above our heads. Initially, a lot of the blokes, including me, thought, Well, that's fucking awesome, they must be coming across us and into the enemy. Then we saw them landing in front of us and realised something was wrong. The Apache fired a second burst that came straight down the ditch on the track we were on. That hit nine of us all in. I started screaming into the radio for the forward air controller to get them to stop, but because of the noise, I didn't know if he was hearing me. I could just see his legs poking out behind a wall and thought he might be dead (I since know he was screaming into his radio for the guy to stop).

I remember thinking, Christ, he's still firing, he can't see us because we're under these trees, I've got to get outside so the Apache can see my helmet and body armour, and maybe he'll stop then because they've got a good zoom on them. Just a split-second decision, I suppose. I got up and ran out into the field to try and wave the helicopter off. Obviously, as a result, I made myself a bit of a target and got shot at by the Taliban, and the Apache fired a third burst as I was getting up. But, thankfully, at that point he heard the radio or got the hint to stop . . . and did.

That was pretty hectic. Things had gone from an outright, overwhelming success, where we could see the enemy we had just killed, to, suddenly, the complete reverse. We had nine injuries, seven walking wounded of various different degrees – shrapnel in their arms or legs. People were bleeding and putting bandages on themselves. Two were seriously hurt. Private Osmond, 'the human sieve', as we called him later, had lots of frag wounds. To be honest, at first I thought he was dead. I thought Private Tatlock was too because he was lying in a ditch, under the water, which was completely red from his blood. He was grey and his eyes had rolled upwards, just showing the white. Private Morris was very brave. He ran about eighty metres across open ground and jumped into the ditch to start treating Tatlock, who was alive, albeit he had been shot in the spine.

I ignored those who were treating themselves and assigned a section commander to each of the two seriously wounded men to treat them and take them back to base – a little over a kilometre away. That took a lot longer than planned. Tatlock couldn't get going because of his spine and Osmond was bleeding everywhere. All of his limbs had been hit and his torso as well. Every wound had to be tourniqued. All this seemed to take a long time, given that we didn't know if the Apache would come back and the enemy had now started firing back at us.

I got on the radio to the FOB and asked for the QRF to come out and bring vehicles, giving them a grid on the map where I wanted to meet them. I needed more troops on the ground to take away our injured and also to provide safety for us all to move back together because at that point we were combat ineffective. I was also aware that I wouldn't be able to stay in command for very long because, quite embarrassingly, I had got hit twice in the left buttock, plus a few smaller pieces in my leg, and I was losing a lot of blood.

I got about halfway back with the last blokes who were protecting the rear and fell over. Private Reynolds and Corporal Desmond bandaged me up when we got to the QRF. It turns out that back at the FOB as soon as these two soldiers, one very young, heard what had happened, they just threw on their helmets, jumped on a quad-bike with a trailer on, and drove through a kilometre of Taliban-controlled territory in order to get there nice and quick. It was brave, so good show to them. I got dumped on the back of this quad and bungeed over the rear-wheel arch. The bloke driving put one arm around me and the other one on the throttle. End of my war.

As it happened, an Italian photographer had arrived that day at the FOB when I was coming back tied to the quad. A few days later, there were a lot of photos in the national press, plus whole-page spreads in the *Telegraph* and the *Mirror* of me hung over the back of this quad bike, covered in blood: 'Blue on Blue in the Valley of Death', said the headline, which made me laugh – and is a good one to have framed in the office.

Everyone always asks what it's like to be shot. Well, it's the impact that hurts at first. In my case it felt like someone

111

had hit me really hard with a golf club – full swing with a driver. But it stopped hurting about ten minutes after they had put a load of morphine in me. When I woke up from my first operation at Bastion, it was bloody agony. I remember coming around from the anaesthetic and the first thought was, Fuck me, that hurts. The nurse said, 'Do you want painkillers?'

'Yes!'

'More?'

'*Yes!*' I've got two scars. One is about ten or eleven centimetres in length, the other is about eight centimetres – angry caterpillars would be the best way to describe them. Except they've got big dents – you could put an egg in either and it wouldn't be seen. They're still painful. Tomorrow, it'll be a year exactly since it happened.

I had two operations in Camp Bastion Field Hospital. Then I got aero med transfer back to the UK and on to Selly Oak Hospital in Birmingham, where I stayed for about twelve days and had a third operation.

I have mixed views about that place, to be honest. Bastion was immaculately clean. Everyone there was military personnel – it is run smoothly along military lines, right through to the transfer. Selly Oak has a military ward in a civilian hospital. If the military aren't filling the beds, the NHS puts civilians in them. It doesn't have enough beds. I woke up in this ward next to an Estonian soldier who'd lost both his legs in an IED attack and diagonally opposite an artillery soldier who'd broken his back in another IED. There was also a civilian bloke who had been in a car crash, and an old fellow with senile dementia – not his fault of course. But in my opinion he shouldn't be on a ward next to a bloke who's just been bombed. That's not right because when you come back, you need to be surrounded by people who understand what you've been through, and know what you're talking about.

The bloke who had broke his back was having a very bad time. He'd be screaming throughout the night with nightmares and stuff and I'd go across on my crutches and talk to him, and that was fine. When he said, 'I was on a patrol in my vehicles,' I understood. The bloke with senile dementia screaming about bananas doesn't have a clue, nor does the civilian.

I had an operation at Selly Oak. The medical staff were very professional, but going down to the operating room on the trolley, I was lying on my front and could see the floor was filthy all along the corridors, and there was dirt in all the corners. It was generally run down – a complete contrast to the immaculate field hospital in Bastion, which in theory you would think would be the worse of the two.

My brother, my mum and dad, and my girlfriend all came up. It was really good to see them, and emotional, certainly for my mum and my girlfriend, who were upset because I'd lost a hell of a lot of weight and I had various scratches and bruises – just silly marks – all over me. Where they'd come from I don't know. Also, I had been taking morphine for two weeks at that point and had had a lot of operations. I imagine I looked a bit of a sorry state, especially as they had seen me on leave a few weeks before, when I'd been quite healthy.

I also had some very good friends who came up to visit, but it was my two best friends who made the most memorable comments. My best mate in the Army just found it funny. Well, I mean, you get wounded in your arse and you can't do anything but laugh. My best civvy friend said, 'Fucking hell, mate, you got what you wished for, didn't you?'

CORPORAL MATTHEW BAKER

'You need to become as one with your wagon...'

I was fourteen when I first started getting in with the wrong crowd. I had lost interest in school, through being dyslexic, not getting any help and being called thick. One summer holiday there were builders in my area. I stuck my head through and said, 'Can I come and work with you?' I built up a rapport with one lad who was a bit older than me, and he became a kind of role model.

Then I found out he was quite a big drug dealer. Basically, he started moulding me into his little workhorse. I was like the drop-off man. My job was ferrying and carrying. He would give me a bag full of drugs, drop me off in the middle of nowhere and say, 'A car is going to meet you and the driver will have a big bag of money. When he's gone, wait five minutes and then phone me, and I'll come and pick you up.' Once that was done, he would put a pile of money in my hand: 'There's your bit, son.' Wow, I had all this money as a young lad and I was going out drinking in pubs before I should. It got to the stage where

115

my mother had a nervous breakdown and I was fighting with my father, who is the straightest, most honest guy in the world.

One day I came into the house and overheard my sister and mum talking. I remember my mum's exact words. 'We've lost our Matty,' she said. She was crying her eyes out. I finally realised what I had done to my parents, and I love my mother and father. That very instant I turned round and took the bus to the Liverpool careers office and joined the Army. One of my proudest moments was when I passed out after fourteen weeks of training. My dad stood at the side of the parade square, and I could see tears streaming down his face. I'd never, ever seen my father cry.

It's coming up to nine years now and I haven't looked back. I have proved to my family I'm not what I was turning into. I went off the rails a bit, but I did come back. I've got a wife now – I'm very happily married and we have a five-month-old little girl. We are not the most well-off people in the world, but at least I know my conscience is clear and I am not a bad person.

I am a driver. I drive the Warrior, which is an armoured personnel carrier. The best way I can describe driving the Warrior is to say it's like being a young kid and going to the fairground for the first time and driving a big go-kart, apart from the turret bars and guns and all that.

The Warrior can carry seven people. Whereas years ago the infantry soldier would be on foot, kit on and off you go, now they're in the back of the Warrior, which saves a lot of blisters on the feet. And you've got armoured cover on the way to the next fight. Bullets are not even going to pierce it. You can hear artillery pinging off the back and you might think, I'm stepping out into that! But at least you haven't had to crawl on your hands and knees five miles up the road while those rounds were coming down on you. The gunner and the commander will see where a position is, take up on the position and section will then bomb-burst out the back. After that the lads will get back in again and the Warrior will pull forward to the next position – that's how you go around the battlefield.

We've got into quite a few firefights and had a couple of hairy moments where we've been pulling RPG tails out of the bar armour. One night we came under very heavy contact and a round just missed the CO's head – it buried itself in his hatch hat on the wagon. I dug it out for him and he put it in his wallet. To be honest, if you go out to Iraq or Afghanistan, unless your job was to stay on the base, you'd be very lucky if you didn't come under contact. Actually, our last tour was a very difficult tour for us. We lost quite a few guys.

When you've driven for a couple of years, you get to know how your commander wants you to drive. You develop a rapport with him – you know what he's going to say before he says it. If he sees an enemy position, you'll automatically know where he wants you to park and at what angle, so he won't have to tell you, 'No, left a bit. No, right a bit, stop, stop . . .' You'll also know how the gunner wants you to drive: if you slam on the brakes and the wagon's rocking, that's longer for him to get sight because the barrels are going up and down. So you must know your wagon, how it's going to stop, what it can do. I know it sounds silly, but you need to become as one with your wagon.

The driver also needs to be able to make the ride comfortable enough for everybody in the back. When you're hurtling along cross country, you've got to watch out for tank holes and ditches and stuff like that because otherwise you are going to end up parking in them. In Iraq you have to drive without any lights on whatsoever and it's pitch black over there. You get used to it – your eyes adapt. But it's difficult terrain. The sidestreets of the towns are open sewers and when you go cross country, it's just sand and bog. Crude oil is laying everywhere. It forms a pool over the top of the sand and if you drive the Warrior into that, it creates suction and you can't get out.

One night there was so much dust around that I completely missed a turning. There was a twenty-foot drop to the side and my wagon clipped it. The road gave way and just my left track was stopping us from rolling down this ravine. I said, 'Everybody needs to get out,' and the seven lads in the back of the Warrior dismounted. They got into a defence position, covering all our arcs in a big circle, because you never know who is watching. I stayed in the vehicle while they got another wagon behind me and tied a rope to the side that was over the edge. As they pulled, I reversed as quick as I could. We finally got it back up and all the lads climbed back in and we carried on going.

It is quite lonely for the driver. You'll be parked up for an hour or more while the attacks go through, and you're like, 'I want to be doing that too' – but all you're doing is being sat there with your body armour and uniform on. You've got this big engine next to you revving away for hours and the heat off that is a hundred degrees of hell. They've started to put small air-conditioning units in the Warriors because it's that hot. Everything metal is hot out there. At midday, when your vehicle is sitting out in the sun, the outer skin is cooking, basically. You need a pair of gloves to climb into it because it would take your skin off if you put your hand on the body. We did the test where we cracked an egg on the front of it. It cooked right through it's that hot. But it's a brilliant vehicle for the infantry, a huge asset, and I don't think we would be without it now.

RIFLEMAN SCOTT BARRS

'Mummy's little soldier . . .'

I was very quiet before I joined the Army, didn't really have a lot of confidence. The Army brought me out of my shell and I became a bit of a character. I'm always smiling now and I like to play practical jokes and have a laugh.

I joined 1st Battalion Green Jackets and soon became a bugler in the signal platoon, which was unusual as traditionally it had been the case that support weapons, i.e. gunners, mortar or anti-tank men, play the pipes, drums or bugles. I didn't know I could play a musical instrument until I was in the bugle store and one of the lads went, 'Here, do you want a go?' I picked it up straight away. The Bugle Major heard me and said, 'Yes, you are a bugler now!' That was it, simple as . . .

My first job was a Remembrance Sunday in Sunderland. I was marching on the second rank behind Corporal Arnold and he told me to shut the eff up because I was playing some crap in his ear. But I have learned a lot since then and hopefully have improved.

Personally, I like doing the 'Last Post' best. As soon as you hear the first two notes, everyone knows what it is. It's incredibly emotional if played correctly. I try to put as much feeling in as I can. But you never get used to performing them. They are very daunting, whether you knew the bloke or not, because everybody is looking at you to give that person a good send-off and it is going to live in their minds for ever if you mess it up.

My first ever 'Last Post' was when I had only been playing a month. They asked me to play for one of the regiment's old boys who had died in Leeds. I warned them, 'I'm no good, but I'll have a go,' but it was horrendous, absolutely hideous. I was cracking notes and rasping everywhere, although everyone came up to me afterwards and said, 'Well done, that was a really good "Last Post".' I think they were just being nice.

I now play in the band full-time because I'm still getting myself back to full fitness after being injured in Iraq in 2006.

It was my first tour of Iraq and I didn't enjoy it from the minute I got there. It's a horrible, stinking, dingy country. I got put into C Company, the support weapons platoon, and found myself being a light machine gunner. I knew all the lads, good lads, every one of them. Each had served over six years, so everyone had good experience.

We were on patrol when a roadside bomb went off, literally over the top of our wagon. It was the first time I had experienced a roadside bombing and I was absolutely terrified. We made a perimeter around the wagons just to see if anything else was happening. Then we mounted back up and drove off. No more than thirty seconds later, another bomb went off and took the engine block out. The vehicle rolled into a wall and threw me out of the back. The wagon was totalled. It had been very close to taking us all out. We were lucky to be alive.

They fired a couple of rounds at us. I picked myself up and sprinted to a corner to get a bit of cover. As I ran, my friend Freedom Myati shouted over, 'Barrsy, will you go back to the wagon and get my ammunition?'

'You can fuck right off!' I said. Bloody cheek.

That night I got to my bed absolutely knackered. About three in the morning the alarms went off. It was a mortar attack and I dove out of bed like a spring chicken. I donned my helmet, put my body armour on and got into a thing called a coffin. It's made of built-up breeze blocks under our beds. The medics were running round treating casualties. I swear I saw this one medic run past wearing just a thong, which was pretty surreal.

Forty-five minutes later the all-clear came through. I went back to bed. For some reason I left my body armour on. Around dawn we heard more mortar rounds going off. The fourth one landed about four feet away from where I was sleeping and knocked me twenty feet across the tent. The body armour took the majority of the blast, but I had massive bits of shrapnel hanging out of my chest. At first they didn't know exactly what injuries I had because they couldn't get my body armour off with all the damage. The serious injury was my arm. I had arterial bleeding in my right arm. My hand was hanging off. I was pretty well in a shit state.

In total seven of us got injured and all from my platoon. I sat next to my mate Mark Kelly, who was a bit shaken up. He had shrapnel and burn wounds to his feet. Somebody walked up and said, 'Do you want a fag?' and he said, 'Fuck off, mate, I've just had smoke inhalation,' which I thought was hilarious. There was a lad called Joe Garton. I thought he was gone – there was hardly anything left of him. My friend Cooper was in bad shape too. My mate Ballsy was just staring at me with his head tilted over. I honestly thought he was dead until he put his thumbs up. It turns out he'd been hit in the arse. That was quite funny when we found out about that.

The ambulance came round and we got CASEVACed on a Merlin helicopter back to the massive field hospital out there. All of us were put in for surgery straight away. I'd broken my wrist, had massive tissue damage and both my lungs had collapsed. They have this thing called chest restraint, where they put a tube into your chest and it inflates somehow. But they have got to break your ribs to insert it. It is extremely uncomfortable and very painful.

It was a bit daunting to telephone my parents and tell them what had happened, but on the same call my sister told me she was pregnant, so that was a bit of good news. My nana then got on the line and said she wanted to come out there and kill all the Germans, which I thought was very funny.

We got mortared while we were in the hospital. That was absolutely hilarious because we were all aching from our injuries and it took us about half an hour either to stand up or sit down. Plus I had a chest drain bag that I had to carry. But as soon as that mortar round landed, we were out of those beds like a swarm, dragging the nurses down with us.

About three days later, I was flown back to Selly Oak Hospital because, with the injuries to my arm, I couldn't hold a weapon. There was no point staying in Iraq.

I had surgery and woke up the next day with my family around me and everybody laughing. I couldn't understand why. 'What are you all laughing at?' It turns out that my mum had baked a heart-shaped cookie, which said, 'Mummy's Special Soldier', and put it above my bed. I got absolutely tortured for that.

Joey Garton was in a bed in my ward and so was Ash, and there was a military padre next to me who had been hit in the shoulder by a mortar round. He was the most foul-mouthed, grumpy old git I have met in my life – and an absolute diamond bloke. Never seen him since, but we shared quite a few laughs in the hospital. He was hilarious and really cheered me up.

Selly Oak was an absolute disgrace. My friend caught MRSA twice in there and you don't catch that twice unless the conditions are absolutely viral. Also, there were civilian patients in with military soldiers, sometimes in our ward. They were getting more care than us soldiers, sometimes for the smallest things. For example, a young girl in our ward had caught her finger in a bus door, which had pulled some of the skin off. Worst of all, the nurses, doctors and military staff there were literally telling us to shut up about our injuries, even though everyone knows the way we soldiers deal with things is to talk about them.

I was in Selly Oak for about a week and home on sick leave for a month. Then I went back to the battalion and they gave me a job to keep my mind off things. I got put in the repat team, doing the 'Last Post'. I buried every one of our lads who got killed in the six months I was over there. Seven were killed and I knew every one of them, which was sickening.

Repatriations are a very hard thing to do, very hard. You would think your emotions would disappear after you'd repeatedly played the 'Last Post', but they really don't, I can tell you. So you mustn't think too much about whoever's just died, otherwise you are going to break down and mess it up.

As soon as you see the feet coming down the Hercules's ramp you start playing. The family is wailing, people are screaming and crying, which could put you off, but you must keep going. The lads in the bearer party do all their drills to get the coffin into the hearse and as soon as the hearse starts to move off, you play 'Reveille'. Then you fall yourself out, march round the back and, nine times out of ten, that's when you break down in tears with all your mates who have just been in the bearer party. You have a cuddle, talk about whoever's just died, have a bit of a laugh, and get on with it.

My battalion, 2 Rifles, are out in Afghanistan at the moment – and we have lost seventeen blokes, which is a massive amount. It's really frustrating that people who are wearing the same cap badge as me are dying because the Rifles are very close. This regiment is a band of brothers. Maybe that's because we are different from everyone else. We wear our uniforms a little bit differently too. We don't have colours – our colours are our cap badge. We are proud to wear everything we have, from the stable belt and the rank slide to the beret. At parade everyone else walks on while we march at the double – 'Swift and Bold' – which is our motto.

CAPTAIN MARK ANTHONY CAPE

'Nothing too good for the Scots Guards . . .'

The 2nd Battalion Scots Guards were preparing for the Major General's inspection, so my boots and tunic were the things that were foremost in my mind. At that moment the commanding officer called us all to the gym and said, 'We're going to the Falklands.'

Where's the Falklands? I knew virtually nothing about the Falklands at that time, except that about a week before, my company commander, had come in to take us for a morning run and stormed into the middle of the Muster Parade, pushing us all out the way. He was holding a copy of the *Sun* newspaper and was shaking with frustration and anger. The headline read: 'Marines Surrender Falklands'. He flashed it in front of the whole company and said, 'While I command Left Flank, that will never happen.' He threw the paper on the floor. We all thought that was kind of funny and took it as a wee bit of a joke, but a week later there we were, in front of the commanding officer. He said, 'Right, we have been given a warning

126

order to form part of 5 Infantry Brigade . . .' At this time, 3 Commando Brigade had already been warned off and we were the follow-up brigade.

Things started to happen very quickly. Within a couple of days, we were away to Brecon to start training for war. Brecon was chosen because it was desolate. Its elephant grass and terrain are quite similar to the Falkland Islands – although it was very warm when we were there, so we didn't experience the cold weather. But it rained a lot and the fields didn't have any irrigation. With all the boots walking on it, it was just a mud bath. The conditions were pretty poor – as a matter of fact, bloody awful.

I distinctly remember: suddenly, for the first time in my military career, the pressure wasn't on me as a soldier, it was on the commanders, who had always put the pressure on me. Also, it was the first time you got respect. In the 1980s nobody gave any respect to young soldiers. Young lads were known as 'crows' and it was, 'Crow, get this, Crow, get that . . .' You were a gopher and you took that as your lot. There was no room for that now. The whole battalion had a totally different ambience, which I thought was exciting. Actually, it felt awesome because suddenly you felt important. And you were important.

We completed Brecon and then had some leave. I went home and, if anybody asked, I was going to the Falklands and I was excited about that. I wasn't going to get shot, somebody else gets shot. I'm indestructible.

But truthfully, we didn't think we were going there to fight. We thought the task force was enough to deal with the Argentinians, that 3 Commando Brigade would have pushed everybody off by the time we got there and wouldn't require any more help. We believed we would be there to garrison a town, true Guards-style – although it was a ferocious brigade, Scots Guards, Welsh Guards and the Gurkhas. It sent a message to the world that we meant business. And Margaret Thatcher did mean business.

After my leave I went back to Chelsea Barracks and prepared to get on a coach to Southampton to sail to the Falklands in the early hours of the following morning. The majority of the battalion went on the town that night, causing a ruckus in all the local drinking establishments, drunk and disorderly, pipes playing everywhere. The following morning the police stations emptied the cells of Scots Guards, although you could see they were still drunk from the night before. The gates in front of Chelsea Barracks were all full of banners from the public: 'Go Get Them, Jocks!' It was all exciting, but we just wanted to get on the ship and get going really.

Well, we chose the *QE2* – nothing too good for the Scots Guards. The *QE2* had been commissioned by the military and a lot of work had been put in to make it war-worthy. The swimming pools had to be taken out and three helipads put in. What I particularly remember about the *Queen Elizabeth* was you always had warm showers, which you didn't necessarily have in barracks, and tea and coffee were on tap whenever you wanted. That was certainly new to us and the food was excellent. Oh, it was very good indeed.

Unfortunately, although we went there as a brigade, most of the brigade assets were taken by 3 Commando Brigade, therefore we knew we were going to have to carry what we needed.

We had to build up to that level of fitness very quickly. We went fitness crazy – it was a quarter of a mile all the way around the ship and we ran the deck for a good two hours every morning, in uniform, carrying weapons and heavy bergens up to ten stone in weight. I remember one ten-stone man stood on a set of scales and his bergen was heavier than him, although, to be fair, he was in the Signals, so he had a lot of spare batteries and ammunition.

The Gurkhas constantly practised the fastest way to get to the evacuation points on the ship – by blindfolding themselves. The rest of us thought it a big joke to grab a Gurkha, spin him round and point him down the stairs so he'd fall down them. The truth of it was, if the ship'd ever gone down, the Gurkhas would have been the only ones who would have made it to the lifeboats, although the water was so cold, you'd be dead pretty quickly if you were to go in.

We got in some serious first-aid training, and weapons training was immense. Competition was high between the sections. Who could carry the most weight? Who could do the fastest weapon drills? Just good fun really, but we felt we were now well trained, although the equipment was a bit of a let-down. Our bergens were just the normal civilian Berghaus bergens and they were creaking with all the weight. The straps snapped quite frequently. In those days we had DMS boots, which stood for 'Dunlop Moulded Sole', but the boot itself was made of compressed cardboard. Great for running in, but not so good for wet conditions.

The weather changed as the ship progressed. We were sunbathing in our shorts until we reached Ascension Island. By the time we got to South Georgia Island, it was just sheets of ice and freezing, bloody horrible. Particles of ice would hit you in the face when you went up on deck.

On 27 May 1982, the *QE2* arrived at South Georgia and the battalion crossloaded on to the *Canberra*, which had GPMGs attached to the side of the deck every two metres – that was the only method of taking out an Exocet missile if one was coming towards the ship. We realised right away we were saying farewell to all the comfort we'd had for the previous two and a half weeks.

The weather now became atrocious. The *Canberra* was going up and down like a yo-yo and so many people were sick, training didn't continue. We had section talks instead. I remember the section commander saying to us, 'Right lads, don't worry, I'll make sure you all come back.' I looked at him and thought, I hope you will. Because we didn't have the right manning level in those days, just before you deployed you'd get a lot of spare people from other units or regiments to make up your numbers. I was starting to ask questions. Is *he* good enough? Would I follow *him*? There were some individuals I wouldn't follow to the Naafi if the pressure was on.

When we arrived, we all formed up in a line with our bergens and dismounted the *Canberra* on to LCUs – old Second World War landing craft. You had to jump from quite a height into the LCUs. That was a bit of a dodgy moment. We had one broken leg dismounting, which wasn't too bad considering. Then we sailed on to the shore at San Carlos Bay on East Falkland.

San Carlos was the beachhead, a desolate and hilly inlet on the north-west of the island, and extremely muddy and difficult terrain. I got up to the hill where I knew my trench was to be dug. My mate Jacko and I marked out the top left-hand trench of the battle group facing that direction and I said, 'Right, just before we start to dig, let's have a cup of tea.' I sat on my bergen. Myself and Jacko had been given thermos flasks and there we were, happy as pigs in poo. We opened up our thermos flasks and *scrch, scrch* . . . they had broken. At that point my morale plummeted. Oh, I nearly cried when I found out my thermos was broke.

We didn't know what to expect at this stage. We were ready to assault, but we were at a secure beachhead, so didn't expect to fight the enemy. We spent three days there, discovering that it was no good to dig a trench because it filled up with water. It was so cold that a number of people nearly went down with exposure. We prepared to move to Bluff Cove on the east coast of the island, but there was a concern that we'd be picked up by the enemy. It was decided that we had to go far out to sea and sneak back in with the LCUs.

We boarded the HMS *Intrepid* and after being fed well by the Navy, had a hot shower – quick, mind you, you couldn't stand there very long. The warm running water was fantastic. In fact, the Navy boys were absolutely brilliant. They'd latch on to you: 'I'll dry your sleeping bag, what else do you need?' We probably didn't respond too well because a number of rogue individuals stole some of their kit from cargo boxes in the hold.

Eventually, we left the *Intrepid*, boarded the LCUs – piloted by the Royal Marines – and proceeded towards Bluff Cove. That was the coldest I've ever, ever been in my life. The wind and rain were lashing straight down on top of us. The waves came up and covered the whole ship with icy water and we froze. So you started the 'Sorry mate, hope you don't mind' routine, where you'd lock your leg in and just cuddle your partner to try and get that extra warmth. It was a survival technique and the manly reluctance to cuddling another soldier disappeared almost immediately.

Meanwhile, our own Navy nearly engaged us, which was quite frightening. One of the ships put up star shells to see who we were and I remember the 2iC screaming to the signals officer, 'Get contact with that ship!' His reply was, 'I can't get contact with the ship,' so then it was, 'Get contact with that ****** ship or I'm going to remove your ****** commission,' and lots of threatening.

We eventually made contact and got them to stop. It was a bloody nightmare.

The Royal Marines brought us into the area where we could land the craft and drop the doorway, and the company commander looked out and said, 'That's not good enough. Get me in further, my men are not getting wet.' We did get wet, but only up to our knees. We were supposed to take over from a company of Paras and secure high ground, but we didn't know where they were. It was dark and we couldn't see if they were dug into trenches.

We unloaded in formations, ready to attack and assault, but nothing, absolutely nothing. Everyone started to freeze once more, so we huddled together again and made a brew to get warm. We sat waiting for the next command as to what to do next. and we waited for morning. The commanding officer was more concerned for the health of the battalion than its ability to mount operations. We were in a pretty bad state and there was quite a high possibility of exposure. However, no rest for the wicked – we were partied to another area, looking for the Paras, when a blizzard hit, soaking us to the skin – normal for an infantry soldier – but hideous.

We got to Bluff Cove by nightfall and built shelters, digging in in case we were attacked. The mindset was: we know we are going to have a fight and the fight is coming soon, we just don't know when. Me and Jacko made an agreement that we would look after each other if one of us was hit, and if one of us was killed, we would speak to each other's families and make sure his things were taken care of.

Every day for just under two weeks, we dug up the turf and peat. We built some formidable positions. Mine had walls six foot high and twelve foot in width, which was absolutely fantastic.

We had a few engagements with aircraft. We claimed one Pucara and a number of Skyhawks that had come in, bombed the *Sir Galahad* and were on their way out, heading back to Argentina. They were combat flying, so only fifty metres off the floor, and flew right over our position, into a wall of fire two kilometres long. They were going to get hit because we did have a formidable machine-gun platoon. When the planes went down, we all jumped up and glorified . . . 'Yeah!'

We killed a sheep. It was gladiatorial. The sheep was dragged in alive, displayed and everybody began chanting, 'Kill the sheep, kill the sheep.' I felt sorry for the animal. It was cooked and then served up, and everyone took a piece – you just hacked off a bit with your knife, put it in your mess tin and ate it. But we didn't cook it correctly and a number of people got ill, dysentery mostly, which was paralysing. I saw a grown man being carried to the toilet. He had no control over his bodily functions: others were queuing to use it after he had been in there. And they wonder why it spread through the whole battalion. We learned by that and stopped killing sheep.

On 13 June we got our orders to assault Tumbledown Mountain. We did our final rehearsals, quite excited. A Marine captain told us how easy the Argentinians were to fight, that they would put up a struggle to start with and then they'd run away because they were conscripts and hadn't got the will to fight. In fact, that was completely wrong information. They weren't conscripts at all. We would be fighting the only regular force of Argentinians on the islands.

Next the assault was cancelled because the attack helicopter was in use elsewhere. We had to postpone it for twenty-four hours. We flew via Sea King helicopter from Bluff Cove to Goat Ridge and dug in. We were mortared all day on the 13th. No deaths, a couple of casualties, nothing severe. We weren't allowed to sleep: sleep provokes thought, which provokes worry. We were ordered to dig all day.

And then in the middle of the night we marched to the start line, quite an awesome sight. That was the first time I'd ever seen the 'Nato T', which is a serious set of lights and torches in the shape of a 'T'. The torches are left to burn and you form up on the T itself. Once you're released from the T, that's you on a compass bearing.

It was a four-phase attack. Around about 1800 hours,

company commander HQ Company led the reconnaissance platoon to the main front and led a diversionary attack to make the Argentinians believe that was where the front assault was going to come from. This assault was actually too successful. They took quite a few casualties, but given there were only twenty men, it was a fantastic achievement.

G Company were to move forward to take out two machine-gun posts. Left Flank, which I was in, were going to follow them through after thirty minutes and take out the main position with whatever tactics were necessary. Right Flank would come up the rear through us and finish off the final position and assault.

H-Hour was 2300 hours. We proceeded towards Tumble-down Mountain only a couple of 'Ks' away. One straight line. Bayonets fixed. Advance. It was quite a feeling to set off on that start line, knowing that I wasn't going to stop until I received a blanket of fire in my direction. Quite unnerving. One kilometre and we would hit the enemy. It was do or die.

That was the idea, anyway. It didn't work like that.

Before I knew it, I fell over somebody. 'Eh, who's that?'

'G Company.'

'What are you doing?'

'The Argies have run away, there's nobody here,' he said.

'All right, OK, keep going.'

Well, they hadn't gone away. They knew we were coming. They had just removed their machine-gun nests and put them in the main position, which Left Flank then took.

We walked on for a further 800 to 1500 metres and came under enemy fire. It was a wall of fire. When you're on the receiving end, it's deafening to hear, a horrible sound called 'crack and thump'. You first hear the crack of the round shooting past your ears and then the thump of the rifle, and the distance between the two of those is how far the enemy sits from you.

We had a lot of casualties in the first couple of seconds. It was the first time I'd ever seen a dead body. The platoon sergeant went. Section commander went, radio operators were getting hit. It was a bit of a free-for-all. The men hit were screaming blue murder until they got morphine. That was absolutely awful, hearing your own men scream.

The enemy were asking us to surrender. We just swore at them. One particular individual was persistent. 'Surrender to the superior Argentinian Forces,' he shouted at us three or four times. Eventually, one of the boys shot him. He lay on the ground screaming his head off, but all you could hear was our lot cheering. That didn't last for long and it was back into the assault again.

Using today's tactics, when you pass a casualty you give him a first-aid bag, make sure he's got his morphine and then leave him because otherwise you lose momentum. Back then we removed the casualties and continued the assault. We lost momentum doing this.

Meanwhile, the company commander was working all the combat power he had available to him: from the ships, from the air, from the ground, on to the front of the position. All that took some time, so we had to wait. Inevitably, just my luck, the covering position I took had water in it. Ice was starting to form on my legs and I couldn't stand. My legs just wouldn't move. I was praying to God we'd be able to move when we needed to.

Finally, the assault went in: three platoons took the attack on the main feature of Tumbledown with one reserve platoon, which I was in.

One platoon ran through the trenches and another took the open ground. They received all the casualties. But the company commander gathered what was left of them and launched them to the top of the mountain. They made it through the enemy and could then see Stanley.

So my platoon was engaged to come forward and take this enemy action out. As we moved forward, I remember passing a friend of mine. He was on the floor. I said, 'Are you all right?'

'Yeah, yeah,' he said.

I crawled up to him and said, 'What's up?'

'I've got no ammunition,' he said. 'I fired all that ages ago . . . aargh.' He thought he was going to die. He was a hardy man, but I gave him a bit of reassurance, and said, 'Don't worry, mate, we're all here, you are now safe.' And off we went.

We moved into forward position. Now I'm sitting at the top of the mountain, and the enemy has fled. I've had a lot of fire coming my way and a lot of people have dropped around me. The section commander came up and said, 'Right, you can relax now.'

Suddenly, I hear something in the rocks and we all go, 'What's that?' Someone asks, 'Who goes there?'

The challenge that night was 'Johnny Johnny', and the answer was 'Jimmy Jimmy', which stood for Johnny the Gurkha and Jimmy the Jock. We fired off with 'Johnny Johnny', but received the same answer back, 'Johnny Johnny', instead of 'Jimmy Jimmy'. We got on the radio and asked if Right Flank had come through at this point. Unfortunately, the radio operator was struck at that very moment and we didn't get an answer back. The people we were challenging were Argies.

The shit hit the fan. We were now being engaged by the enemy. Hand grenades came in. The section commander was hit and the Section 2iC fell to the floor, no movement at all. All that's left now were five Guardsmen and we were screaming lunatics, engaging anything that moved, 360 degrees, until we took control among ourselves.

The enemy withdrew, but the section commander kept screaming and screaming. Most of his face had gone from the explosion. We pulled him down because he was giving away our position. We managed to get an injection of morphine into him and that calmed him down.

We were now leaderless. The section commander had gone. The company commander shouted out, 'What's going on?'

One of us said, 'Well, the section commander and 2iC are both casualties.'

'Right,' he said. 'Remain there till daylight.' That wasn't really what I was wanting to hear, but OK, we can stay there. Praying and praying for daylight to arrive. We waited for Right Flank to come through. I'm sitting there on my rock, shivering a bit. I ate a biscuit. I just wanted to see it to the end. I wouldn't say I was a religious man, but I was that night. I was too young to die.

Meanwhile, Right Flank were assaulting and coming through. I could see them approaching me in a straight line.

Even though I knew that was Right Flank, I thought, Better challenge them, as we had already been let down by a challenge procedure. I couldn't trust my own feelings any more. So we went, 'Johnny Johnny', and they never answered. And I thought, Right, that's it. I screamed, 'Right Flank, if you don't answer our challenge, I am about to engage with a general-purpose machine gun.' And one of the two commanders piped up and said: 'Yes, totally right, it's Right Flank. Where is the enemy?'

'Look right,' I said. 'You'll see the muzzle flashes, that's your enemy. OK?' I quickly pointed him on to the enemy.

He never did say 'Jimmy Jimmy'. And he didn't leave us a medic either. 'We're keeping him,' he said, and off they trundled to finish the rest of the attack. Unfortunately for Right Flank, they took a lot of casualties. They went over too quick and didn't check all the positions. As they went past, enemy were popping up behind and taking them on.

We could now see the Marines and Paras all racing into Stanley, but although the flags had gone up, we were still being engaged by individuals. There was a lot happening. We had stretcher parties being taken out by mortars. We had prisoners of war to take care of, our own casualties and dead to pick up.

We took the dead back to the re-org area, where the sergeant major took control. Our casualties were being slowly but surely evacuated by the one helicopter that would come forward to us. We didn't bring the enemy dead back.

Enemy lay in every single trench. As we went round, we rifled their kit. They had been better equipped than us, including having amazing night-vision goggles. We took their food and cigarettes and rounded up the last of the prisoners of war. I remember two boys left in a trench, dead bodies around them. They were just trembling. All their friends had died. They were frightened children really. I was young myself, but looking at those two, I really felt sorry for them. We pulled them out and treated them as you would a prisoner of war: we gagged and disoriented them, but I felt at that point, What's the point? I don't want any information from them: we've won, the boys are in Stanley already.

Finally, the war was over. It was done.

We all went on a battlefield tour and retraced our steps of the previous night. The difference between night, when you're on your belt buckle crawling round, and daylight, when you're standing up, is immense.

We stayed overnight on the mountain, which we needed to do, taking stock, trying to get our thoughts together really. You can't take somebody from a battlefield and put him into normality. You have to bring him down slowly. Leaving us on the mountain for an extra twenty-four hours was a good thing.

We had our bergens back and warm clothing. Everyone was happy because we were alive. We were all talking together. We told each other some wild stories:

'Oh, I nearly got these two . . .'

'I killed four . . .'

'I was under machine-gun fire for thirty minutes solid . . .'

The tales were increasing in valour, just like fishing stories, you know, but they were relatively true.

When it went dark again I had a scare. Everybody smoked

and people were flicking away their cigarettes. Seeing the ends go through the air was frightening and unsettling: it was just like a round at night when you were being shot at, but with no noise. Very unnerving.

Finally, we were helicoptered to a barn in Fitzroy, where the quartermaster fed us. He had an all-in stew, just basic stuff really, but it was appreciated more than any five-star hotel. The pipers piped us into the barn, which was fantastic. Well, it's traditional in the Scots Guards. A piper also takes his pipes into battle and we had demanded the pipes to play when we were assaulting. Unfortunately our piper's reeds had gone missing, so he couldn't play, and he got roundly abused for that.

We met our other companies at last. It was great to be back home again with the battalion family. That's how we looked at it. Mind you, now there was heat: when our feet started to thaw out, you heard screaming all night because the pain was immense.

Although the island had surrendered, Argentina hadn't. We had to wait and see if they were going to come back at us. We prepared defensive positions around Port Howard on West Falkland, but in a little less stressful state now. We occupied houses, where we could cook hot food and be in a dry environment with four walls, a roof and a fire that heated the whole house. Plus the odd tot of whisky was getting thrown around. But the longer we stayed the more frustrated we became. When were we going home? We stayed for a further month, the last soldiers there. I'd have argued that since the Scots Guards were the only ones to engage the enemy, maybe we deserved to leave earlier.

We helped the local community, mending fences and digging pits. We also began to clean up all the Argentinian mess. There was ammunition absolutely everywhere. The Falklanders are lovely people. You get the fullest hospitality. All their doors are open and you are free to go into another man's house. The Falkland Islands are similar to parts of Belfast, although without the aggressive streak. The Queen's portrait is in every living room.

Eventually, we flew back into Brize Norton and got the bus to Chelsea Barracks. That was bad. People were cheering us along the road, but somebody showed a backside to them from the back of the bus and someone else flicked a v-sign – very unlike the coach ride to Southampton when we were waving back. But we didn't care for anybody else. We only cared for ourselves: if you weren't Scots Guards, you were nothing. That was the attitude.

My mother said the Falklands had changed me, that I came back a totally different person. To be honest, I couldn't wait until my leave finished and I could get back to my unit. It was a little bit unfair to my family and friends, but at that time you only respected those people you had served with.

I have spent several years in Northern Ireland and in Iraq, but nothing competes with the Falklands in terms of aggressive, short, fast, hand-to-hand fighting. The Falklands was the last domain of that kind of battle. They have different battles today. Yes, you are fighting, you are engaging at point of bayonet with the enemy – but you've got lots of ammunition, your food's good, your clothing's good, mail's getting through, you're communicating all the time, you have a mobile phone. In the

Falklands, you were on survival mode from the moment you went. There was no communication. You could only take what ammo you could physically carry – people threw ammunition away because they couldn't carry it. What was more important, the heavy weight you were carrying or your life?

Some of us have been asked to go back, but I don't think I'm ready yet. I'll go back when I am not a serving soldier any more. That is the time when I will go back to the Falklands and not before.

WARRANT OFFICER CLASS I (RSM) PAUL DOWNES

'Kiwi is the secret . . .'

Ever since I was a child, when anyone asked, 'What are you going to do when you grow up?' I'd reply, 'I'm going to be a soldier.' When I was sixteen, I called at the recruiting office in Coventry, where I'm from. I'm a tall fellow, six foot five inches, and the recruiting sergeant said, 'You're made for the Guards Division.' He gave me a few leaflets. And the more I read them, the more that's what I wanted to be. Being an Englishman, I didn't fancy the Scots, Irish or Welsh Guards, so I joined the Coldstream Guards, which is a good English regiment. And here I am now, forty years old, and still in. I've got another fifteen years, and if I finish at fifty-five, I will have spent the majority of my life in uniform.

The Coldstream Guards have been around for ever. We can trace our history back to Oliver Cromwell and the New Model Army. Every regiment in the British Army is unique, and every person in that regiment will tell you they're the best, but in my opinion, *we* are the best. Every man in our regiment wants to be there and is dedicated to the cause. It doesn't matter where we go on operations, the reports that come back are glowing because we will always put in 100 percent, and we'll do it 'Second to None', *Nulli Secundus*, which is our motto.

I'm in charge of the Army School of Ceremonial, which teaches instructors how to teach drill to both recruits and the wider Army. Learning to march, and reacting to orders and commands, forms the basis of military discipline. A lot of the ceremonial drill movements we carry out today stem from the battlefield. Trooping the Colour, for instance. In the past, before going into any battle, the colour was paraded in front of the regiments for everybody to be fully aware of what their colour looked like, so that in the confusion of battle it could be a rally point.

All the instructors at the All Arms Drill Wing are Guardsmen, purely because the Guards Division has the depth of knowledge and experience. It's just one of those things. The Guards are the experts at drill: Trooping the Colour, Guards of Honour, you name it, the boys have done it. When the Guards units come back from an operation, they'll put on their red tunics and bear-skins, and after a couple of weeks of training, they'll be good to go – they can turn their hands to everything.

The first thing a recruit learns is how to stand to attention, and then how to stand at ease. You progress to marching, and build in the movements. They learn how to turn to the left, then to the right, then about turn, and saluting on the march. A good salute should see the right arm raised sideways taking the longest route up from the position of attention and at the end of the salute taking the shortest route down to the side of the body.

The hand should be flat, fingers fully extended, one inch above the eye – basically, you touch your cap badge if you are wearing a beret. These aren't difficult things to pick up. It's practice makes perfect. I always say to the instructors, 'Drill is like sex. The more you do it, the better you become,' which always gets a laugh.

My first ever ceremonial duty in London as a young Guardsman was as a sentry at St James's Palace. If you're where the tourists are, you can watch the ladies go past, which is a definite perk. But it can be quite arduous stagging on. If you've got a poor-fitting bearskin, it can dig into the side of the head. If it's towards the end of the day, and there's no one around or it's raining, it does get pretty dull and boring.

When I first joined, we used the old SLR rifle, which was long and rested on the floor, but the SA80 rifle we have now stays in the hand at all times. It becomes quite heavy after you've been stood still for about fifteen minutes. Hence why we have various movements: you can change arms and you're allowed to march fifteen paces to the left or right when on sentry duty, to stretch your legs and keep the blood flowing.

When you're on parade you want to look smart, and the first thing the public look at with the Guards Division is shiny boots. You can clearly tell if someone's bothered to clean their shoes or not. Kiwi is the secret. Don't use anything else. You brush-polish the shoe completely to get all the grit and dust off, plus the flakes that come off on the natural bend in the leather. Then you have two different tins of polish, one for layering up and one purely for what we call 'bulling'. To layer up, apply a thin film of polish with your fingers until it's smooth and hard. Leave it to dry for forty-five minutes, maybe an hour. Then get what we call a 'sylvet', which is used to clean silver, put your fingers in, two or three fingers – I tend to use three just as a personal preference – then a dab of polish, and off you go, small circles, not too heavy a pressure; you're bulling the toecaps, all the uppers and also what we call 'the wood', which is the sides or edges of the sole of the boot, because if they're dull, it doesn't finish the boot off.

I've done Trooping the Colour several times now and at various different ranks. The best one was being a company sergeant major in London District. I have a photograph of myself where I've gone past Her Majesty, eyes right, saluted her, and I'm literally six feet away from her – the closest man out of my company. Being that close to Her Majesty, well, I don't think I can really describe the feeling. That was the culmination of six weeks' training, Monday to Friday, to get to that standard: the sweat, the aching, the screaming and shouting and controlling of your men to get them right, just so that when we marched past Her Majesty in two ranks of thirty-three men abreast on that day, she could look down the line and see that each rank was perfectly straight. We all looked her in the eye as we gave her an 'eyes right' and marched proudly past. And when it goes well, you get a massive sense of achievement and pride. After all, she is the Colonel-in-Chief of the Coldstream Guards, the finest regiment in the Household Division and the Army. Irrespective of the regimental rivalry in the Household Division, I think that all Guardsmen see themselves as Her Majesty's personal troops and are therefore incredibly loyal to the royal family. We are as proud today when taking part in ceremonial events such as the Trooping of the Colour as were our forebears who did it before us.

A couple of weeks later, you always get a letter from Her Majesty to all the units involved, stating exactly what she thought of the parade.

There are contingencies in place for when a member of the royal household dies. It's just a case of pulling up the relevant file. They are very complex documents and a lot of prior planning has taken place in order to get all the detail correct. There are various units from the services whose patron she is, who would be involved in the funeral, and who would obviously have to be trained. I would go straight down to London with three of my instructors to assist the Garrison Sergeant Major of London District in the preparation of the troops for the parade. There'd be things like street-lining to organise and the lying in state of the coffin in Westminster Cathedral. We would assist the Yeoman Warders and Officers who would guard the coffin during the vigil, covering such things as how to move into position and conduct the changeover procedure correctly.

There're a lot of things that are totally unique to funeral drill; the soldiers will do what we call staff or levy drill, where they'll slide their feet as opposed to stamping their feet, and what is called reverse arms and lower on your arms reverse.

One of my main roles at the moment is to go down to RAF Lyneham and conduct the repatriation ceremony for the bodies of those soldiers killed in Afghanistan and Iraq. The aircraft they use is a C-17 Globemaster, which is one of the RAF's new transport aircraft and it is a big old bird. When the aircraft comes to a halt, the ramp will be lowered, and as the families are brought out into the marquee by the senior officers, I march the bearer parties, who have already formed up under my command, on to the rear of the aircraft. I then take position at the bottom of the ramp, and as soon as I see everyone is in the marquee, a nod of the head is the signal for the bearer party to come forward and enter the aircraft. They march up the ramp and into the aircraft. It takes approximately ten minutes per coffin to remove it from the aircraft and march it around to where the hearse is located opposite the family members in the marquee, and also opposite the aircraft. Repatriations that involve multiple bodies, and I have conducted two ceremonies where there have been five coffins on the aircraft, can take up to fifty minutes to complete. The important thing is to try and get the ceremony completed as quickly as possible without cutting corners, but without prolonging the agony for all the family members concerned who are watching. I always conduct thorough rehearsals the day before and on the morning of the ceremony. It can be difficult at times for many of the young soldiers who have to take part in the ceremony and they sometimes get quite emotional themselves during it and afterwards. Invariably they will have known the deceased very well and you have to give words of encouragement before the ceremony to keep the guys focused. To a man they have never let me down, which is testament to their training, pride and professionalism.

On the odd occasion, maybe at the pub for instance, someone will ask, 'Have you killed anyone?' I don't say yes, I don't say no. I think to myself, Why are you asking that? Why do you want to know? I mean, it's like me asking you when did you lose your virginity. It's private, isn't it? How would people react if I said, 'Yes, killed loads.' It would stop the conversation dead, excuse the pun.

'Would you be prepared to kill?' Well, that's a different question. 'Yes', because that's what I'm trained to do and if I don't shoot the enemy, he's going to shoot me. When you get down to the bare bones of it, if you're not prepared to kill an individual who's shooting at you, how good are you going to be to the rest of the team?

To tell the truth, people of my age haven't killed that much. You may get the odd soldier who was involved in an incident in Northern Ireland where they may have been very lucky and shot and killed an IRA terrorist, but the 'Olds and Bolds', as we call ourselves, haven't got as much fighting experience as some of the young soldiers coming in now. If you talk to the kids who have done a tour of Iraq and Afghanistan, it's 'Yeah, yeah, we killed twenty people.' You'll find soldiers who have been four or five years in the Army and they've got more fighting experience than I have in all my twenty-five years. In some ways it makes me wish I could have all my time again because if you ask any soldier – well, infanteer for sure – if they're totally honest, every soldier would say, 'Yes, I want to go and do what I was trained to do,' as frightening and as daft as it may sound. They want to put their training into perspective on the battlefields actually to see: have I got what it takes?

I've seen my fair share. I have been on plenty of Northern Ireland tours, a United Nations tour of Bosnia and I was a mortar fire controller in the first Gulf War. I just missed a tour of Afghanistan with my regiment because I was promoted into a post to train instructors at Catterick, but we are gearing up to go again. I've just commissioned. I move back to be a captain in my regiment later on this year.

If you want the Army for a career, it's fantastic. I've been all round the world – few people have got around the world as much as I have. I went to Hong Kong for two years. I've been to Australia, South Africa, Fiji Islands, Borneo three times, Canada twice. I served in Germany for six years and most recently I was fortunate enough to be sent to Tonga to advise the Tongan Armed Forces on drill for the King of Tonga's coronation ceremony. I have been fortunate to have a full and varied career so far. I have been all over the world and have been trained to fight in many different types of warfare. I've done the normal infantry stuff. I am a jungle warfare instructor and have taught in Belize. I am a mortar instructor. I have taken part in armoured warfare and tested my skills in real operational theatres in Northern Ireland, Bosnia and the Gulf War. The only thing I haven't done, and would have loved to have done, is Arctic warfare.

SERGEANT MAJOR JIMMY FITZWATER

'Put out of action, nullify, neutralise, subdue or destroy the enemy...'

I didn't join straight from school because I truanted a lot and my father said if I didn't knuckle down he wouldn't sign the papers for me to join as a boy soldier. You need to have parental consent to join under the age of eighteen. I didn't mend my ways and, true to his word – he wasn't a man to make idle threats – he didn't sign the papers and I joined the Merchant Navy instead, aged sixteen.

The Merchant Navy is a general term for any sort of boat that moves goods from A to B. It's like lorry-driving on boats. You've got the great big oil tankers run by well-established companies like Shell and BP, and at the other end of the spectrum, you have the shitty little rust-buckety type of things that mainly trawl coal, wheat, grain and steel from the Continent and around the UK. I worked on one of those.

The ship was owned by a cowboy entrepreneur. His turnover of crew was high because the pay wasn't very good and the

152

conditions weren't that great either, but it was a job. I became a deckhand and learned to cook full meals instead of just beans on toast. It was a hard, man's world. There were no allowances for a boy – the first time I burned the dinner, I got a punch in the head for it. But the camaraderie between the blokes who worked on the ships was really good and I was just having a great time. You can imagine: Amsterdam and Rotterdam, whorehouses, late-night drinking …

I was going along happily in the Merchant Navy past my eighteenth birthday. What revitalised me was a programme on the telly following a Para platoon through training. Coincidentally, the Falklands War kicked off while it was being filmed, so of course they linked it all together – great from a journalistic point of view. Cor blimey, they couldn't have planned it better. That was the first time I thought, I want to join the Paras, because until then I had only wanted to join the Army.

We went to Brize Norton to learn how to jump out of areoplanes – which is what Paras do. You've got to drive yourself straight out into the slipstream so you don't end up twisted or bent over. You learn what to do if you have a malfunction or if one of the many things that can go wrong does go wrong. Avoiding other people is more luck than judgement when there're ninety blokes all leaving an aircraft at the same time – that's a lot of blokes in the air. With military parachuting you are very confined in the aircraft, plus you're sweating like nothing else because you've got on your helmet and all your kit and you're nervous. You've really got the butterflies going. Also, the jump is usually preceded by two or three hours' low-level tactical flying, which is ten times worse than seasickness. Blokes are throwing up everywhere and if you are not throwing up yourself, the sound and smell of everyone else being sick makes you want to throw up.

My first operation, apart from the tours of Ireland (of which there were many), wasn't until I'd been in the Army for about fifteen years. It was in Sierra Leone.

Do you remember the incident where soldiers from the Royal Irish Regiment got captured by the West Side Boys? There was a massive hullabaloo with the British government. A Royal Irish contingent was out there training the Sierra Leone Army and a group of renegades captured a bunch of our lads. The group called themselves the West Side Boys. A bunch of drug-addled thugs basically, they used to take locals and imprison, rape and do all sorts of horrible things to them. A Royal Irish patrol was in the Okra Hills, out in the bundu, and these thugs fancied their chances, I suppose. Two wagons full of their blokes seized eleven Royal Irish soldiers and made these ridiculous demands before they'd give them back. They wanted transistor radios and engines for their blooming canoes. One of the leaders of this group, a self-styled brigadier who was an ex-corporal in the Sierra Leone Army, demanded something along the lines of: 'I will let them go, if you make me President of Sierra Leone.' Through negotiation with the British government, half of the soldiers did get released, but the West Side Boys held on to the others. The government directed that a rescue package be put together for the rest and this required some support from one of the Para companies. That was to be us.

We were back in England at that moment, and it was just before a mess function actually, so we were all dolled up in our mess kit, when the OC called us in and said, 'Make sure the blokes get packed, you are going to be deployed somewhere.' Everyone guessed exactly where we were going, but because of operational security nobody could say directly.

The very next morning we went to South Cerney and got bombed up, bullets and ammo and all that, and flew out to Senegal. We were there for a night, then flew into Sierra Leone under cover of darkness. Then we jumped into a four-tonner, all of us in the back, canopies down, and drove on to a ramshackle car ferry, across a wide estuary, on to this camp in the middle of the bush. Hastings Camp it was called. Typical bush camp. Loads of tents, perforated baked bean tins for showerheads, communal shitters and 'desert roses' – lengths of plastic pipe for pissing into, dug at an angle into the ground and sticking out up to groin height. The idea is that the pee soaks into the ground below the surface, therefore avoiding stench and disease, but imagine two hundred blokes in a confined camp in a tropical country, each pissing four or five times a day . . .

Before you go into any battle you have a set of orders. The hostages had to be rescued. Our mission was to attack and, in so many words, put out of action, nullify, neutralise, subdue or destroy the enemy. Of course, battles never go according to plan – there's a saying in the Army: 'No plan survives contact with the enemy.' In other words, as soon as the first rounds go down, the plan goes to rat shit. But having a plan is better than having no plan.

Prior to actual contact with the enemy, there was a huge amount of nervousness because apart from bits and pieces in Northern Ireland, this was my first enemy contact. Although you've practised for years and years, nobody knows how they are going to react in battle. Are you going to crack up or freeze, or choke? There are stories of people who everybody thought would be fantastic on the battlefield who weren't, and other people who were thought to be fannies who did the business very well. Until somebody tries to shoot at you and kill you, you don't know how you are going to react. You train for it, you can be as prepared for it as you like, but you don't know. The main hope going through your mind is that you don't let yourself down.

And then, finally, at dawn we were helicoptered by Chinooks – the great big ones with two rotors on top – into the camp village where the hostages were. Actually, there were supposed to be three Chinooks, but one had developed problems, so we had three chopper-loads of blokes squeezed into two choppers.

What happened next was: the enemy were sleeping in their beds, when all of a sudden their morning is interrupted by .50 cal heavy machine-gun fire blasting from two helicopters into their camp, the sound of two enormous choppers landing and a shitload of blokes charging out the back. They'd all crashed out in a drugged and drunken stupor from their party the night before. You can imagine their panic and everything: blokes just rushing out, grabbing their weapons and trying to shoot back with one hand while wiping the sleep from their eyes with the other hand.

Once the rounds started going down, your training does kick in. You remember what you have practised and trained for all these years and you just do it. It's like driving a car: you don't think about what your foot's doing on the pedal or what your hands are doing on the gear stick, and how you coordinate the two actions, you just do it automatically.

I remember seeing my first casualty. It was one of my blokes, Private Wilson, the platoon radio operator, who had only joined six months before. Wilson was holding a field dressing to himself and blood, real blood, was pouring out. I remember the colour of his face, all sort of pale and grayish, from shock, basically. 'Fuck me, I've been shot,' he said. And running past him, I was thinking, Bloody hell, he's been shot! Maybe I was waiting for the next rake of gunfire to come my way, but also that was the moment I finally realised, Shit, this is real, this is not training any more.

Something else that still sticks in my mind: there was a wide dirt track running through the village and in the middle of this road was a pair of Caterpillar boots, laid perfectly neatly together, like somebody had just come out and daintily put them down and wandered off. I remember it going through my mind, How the fuck did those boots end up like that? Because with everyone running around like blue-arse flies, you would expect kit to be scattered everywhere, a single boot on its side or maybe one boot ten metres from the other. I still can't figure it out.

By the time we got on the choppers to go, the enemy were gone, dead or fled, there was no one there any more. I suppose the main feeling was elation. 'That was fucking great, wasn't it?' Knowing nods, looks and smiles to each other as if to say, 'I did it, I didn't crumble under pressure.' In the evening we drew offshore to a royal fleet auxiliary ship, the *Sir Percival*, and we had a few beers in one of the mess rooms. I had two cans and I was then so tired, well, I can't describe how tired I was, you come down off an adrenalin rush like that and there's nothing left.

That was a very quick op, in and out. You barely had time to think. But blokes in Afghanistan are there for six months and in firefights almost daily. I don't know how they do it. That's bound to have an effect on someone.

I'm forty-three now. I would have loved to be involved in ops a bit more because the thing is, once you have tasted it, you want more. It's like anything that gives you an adrenalin rush, dangerous sports for instance – why do so many people engage in dangerous sports? I suppose ops are the realisation of all the things that attracted me to the Army in the first place: bullets flying around, crawling on your belt buckle and shooting at people, and people shooting at you. However, you can't dwell too much on missed opportunities and I thank Fate I got on one operation out of twenty-two years in the Army. Some people have gone through their whole career and not seen any ops, just loads of tours of Northern Ireland.

When blokes are putting their lives on the line like that, it changes them. I suppose it made me value my life more and also get more annoyed at people who whinge and moan about inconsequential things. 'I haven't got enough make-up.' 'There's no hot water.' Things that don't matter, they are not life or death situations. A bloke died on that op, blokes got injured, some seriously, and people just complain about shite.

Being a soldier has a big influence on your married life, probably a negative influence from the wife's perspective. The Army says you are going and you go – by the time my children were four and five, we had moved seven times. The wife, Kathy, she's not just a housewife, she is a professional woman, a general registered nurse. With all our moving, she can never settle into a job or make any career progression. I go off for six months to

Northern Ireland or on exercise for three or four weeks, and it's great, I'm having a good old time with my mates and my blokes while she's left at home with the kids to fend for herself.

Because she's not caught up in the whole military thing, Kathy doesn't ask much about what I do. For example, she doesn't know any of the things I've just told you. The first thing she said to me when I came through the back gate after Sierra Leone was something like 'Did you enjoy yourself, then?' Obviously she needs to work on her interview technique!

Some people argue the toss – maybe because they are in denial – but I think if you make a career in the Army, then the Army comes before your family because if the Army didn't come before your family, when your wife said, 'I don't want you to be in the Army any more,' you'd get out.

Every now and again it comes up again. You know, 'You've always put the Army before me and the kids . . .' I can't then turn round to her and say, 'You are right, I have put the Army first.' You have to say, 'No, I don't.' But I know it and so does she – the Army comes first.

MAJOR CHRIS FRAZER

'The world according to Frazer . . .'

Before battle the men will be getting on with their tasks. They'll be with their mates in little gaggles, having a coffee, a soft drink or a smoke. They're all on the same wavelength, tuned into each other, and focused on the job to be done.

The relationship between a commander and his men has got to be nurtured. It is based on trust and confidence, such things as knowing Christian names (but not using them), knowing the names of wives or girlfriends and when their children's birthdays are, bits and bobs like that, all go towards establishing that trust. Then they can look at you and think, Well, he actually knows an awful lot about me, he cares about me, therefore he's not going to sacrifice my life in vain.

You've got a million jobs to do and a million and one things to think about. You spend an awful lot of time making sure your preparations are the best they can be, talking to all kinds of different people to give you as much information as possible.

For instance, the intelligence officer will have established a number of links with the local community and police. He is responsible for getting all these little snippets of information, which on their own bear no relevance but when added together and analysed become intelligence. For instance, at first I didn't think much of one comment – 'Always watch the roofs' – because the heat of the summer was just horrendous and people in the towns and villages would sleep on the flat roofs. Then we realised that the enemy were using them as a thoroughfare – hence we would watch the roofs.

I'll talk to the Engineers. They are good people. I have a huge respect for the Engineers. They are awesome. We had a really good battle group Engineer, who'd be there on all offensive or defensive operations to clear through minefields and conduct route recces to make sure the ones we were using were capable of sustaining heavy movement. He made sure we had the resources necessary if we needed to dig in or site a bridge to cross a river.

I'll talk to the tanks. I had seven Challenger tanks from the Royal Armoured Corps, which is half a squadron, and that's a pretty big force multiplier: you've got seven 120mm guns, each with fifty-two rounds, and a significant amount of firepower in addition to the main armament above that as well, plus, they've got a monster V12 engine, which you can hear for miles when the turbines kick in. Close up you can feel the ground shake as they rumble past – and the Iraqis just knew that if they started anything kinetic, they were going to get it back in spades.

If you're in the poo and really need somebody to come and help you, then I'd want helicopters every time – the Apaches flown by the Army Air Corps are the best, so I'll talk to them. I would also talk to the air – their Harriers, flown by the Royal Navy, bless them, at five hundred-odd miles an hour, with five-hundred-pound bombs strapped either side of their wings, do illustrate a significant statement of intent. But if you're trying to win the hearts and minds of the people you need to be accurate with your target selection, we must stop causing unnecessary collateral damage. We keep saying to the local indigenous population, 'We're a force for good,' but then all of a sudden we smash their houses or their wells, kill all their livestock, trash their crops, and although assistance payments are made, they initially think, Well, hang on, there's no way I'm now going to be able to earn an income, so tell me how you're a force for good? – leaving them little option but to pick up a weapon. All you do by killing an individual is cause another ten who were possibly neutral to turn against you – we're seeing a similar phenomenon in UK cities like Bradford, Luton and others with a wide cultural mix – they feel ostracised because of the stigma attached to their religion. We have to be cleverer in our approach: we need to address the reasons why people are choosing to fight, not just going in and fighting them.

The politicians say we are winning – and they are right, we are inflicting a high level of attrition against the enemy, they're killing them in droves. But the madrasahs in Pakistan and Baluchistan are filling up with these young boys and girls who have been indoctrinated into the whole 'We must fight for the good of the Islamic world against the Western oppressors' argument.

No matter how good a plan is, if it is not underpinned by a robust, workable logistic plan it will fail, so I'll talk to logisticians. They provide truckers and cooks. You have to ask yourself why anyone would want to be a military chef. Working in the kitchens in fifty degrees of heat, compounded by the heat of the ovens on top of that, I have massive respect for chefs. Those guys are getting the boys' food, which is one of the few things they have got to look forward to during the day. With very little resources the chefs make the meals as appealing and appetising as possible, despite the fact that we had dehydrated food to start out with – somebody had sent out a load of dehydrated rations. The thing is, in a theatre like Iraq, you've got to consume between six and twelve litres of water a day just to keep yourself alive, and that's without washing and shaving and keeping your clothes clean. The moment you need more water, your poor private soldier has got to drive a huge wagon of water up that corridor, and he's taking an unnecessary risk, and so you're thinking, Don't give us dehydrated food – thankfully it was addressed, but people need to consider the unintended consequences of their actions.

Finally, I'll talk to aviation for CASEVAC, so we have the necessary wherewithal and assets in place should we need to get a casualty extracted to a recognised and full-on, fully equipped medical facility, so the men know that if they get hurt they will receive the very best medical attention you can give them.

Because of the technical and physical assets we've got, the odds are stacked in our favour. But the bottom line is that the enemy, the insurgent, whatever you want to call him, only has to be lucky once. He doesn't care if he's shot because he wants to be a martyr. He wants to go to paradise with the fifty million virgins and all the rest of it. If he dies in a hail of bullets it matters not. But it matters to Frazer and my men. So I have to be confident that everything is as complete as I possibly can make it. It's not risk assessment because that's a civilian term but I have to be sure that I've used my experience and knowledge to reduce the risks – not to an acceptable level because there'll never be an acceptable level – but to a manageable level. So when we cross that line the odds remain favourable. And that's all about preparation and that starts by considering the most minute detail, something as innocuous as making sure you watch the roofs, which, in the end, has absolutely huge significance.

With infrastructure rebuilding in Iraq, getting pumping stations operational again, putting up buildings, and so on, we'll try and use workers from the host nation because then you are putting money back into the local economy – although as we don't know what the going rate is, the local contractor will pull our pants down every time and inflate his costs considerably – this is frustrating, but it is a fact of life in certain countries.

Majar Al Kabir is an absolutely hideous, evil place, with a real menacing undertone of pure violence and hatred. We'd had all sorts of issues there and were trying to settle the place down. Colonel Mark Castle, my boss, moved heaven and earth to get the hospital this monstrous great generator that came from the World Bank, or somewhere like that. This bloody thing was massive, much bigger than they needed, it could have run the whole town. Now we could say, 'We're not just Western invaders or crusaders, or whatever you want to call us, we're here to make your life better.' Having installed the generator, we expected the town council to be pleased, even grateful, but no, they said, 'How are we going to fuel it?' You're thinking, Well, fellas, we've just given you this gift, you're sitting on the second biggest reserve of oil in the world . . . take a wild stab in the dark how you are going to fuel it? Do you want your hospital to have power? Do you want your X-ray machines to work? Do you want the air-con to work? Do you want your people to get better?

We had literally millions of dollars stored in an ISO container in Camp Abu Najir because the whole economic structure of Iraq had collapsed. Apart from stealing things off each other and the fractured state, they had no way of generating an income. A friend of mine was paying money to these Iraqi Army guys in the football stadium in Al Amarah. There were about six thousand of them, all waiting, and it was taking a bit of time to pay all these people. It was getting hotter and hotter. They were becoming really fractious.

We had a company of our blokes in public order kit there, but it didn't make any difference. The mood and patience of the crowd was worsening and they knew we Westerners would not fire on them – whereas the old regime would have just hosed them down if the situation had gotten out of control, which was why demonstrations were pretty few and far between in the Saddam era. The only thing that worked for us was to bring forward an attack dog, well, they're not called attack dogs, they're called patrol dogs, but if you let them off the lead they'll bite any bugger, including their handlers. 'Land sharks', we called them. When a great big snarling, salivating Alsatian, weighing about eight stone, went forward it was literally like the parting of the Red Sea because the crowd knew what the dogs would do and they were afraid. It did calm the situation down and they did get paid eventually.

I was very pleased to leave Iraq. I thought it was a horrible place. Nothing you could do for those people was ever enough.

The temperatures in the summer were phenomenal. They were horrendous. They have a hard old life, same as the Afghans. The average life expectancy is forty-five, fifty, in both countries. This is why religion is a key to them. They are told by the mullahs and others that they will be going to a better world after they pass through this one, and they look forward to that – it's why they are happy to give their lives so freely in battle because they truly believe that they are off to a better place.

Spending time in Iraq and Afghanistan has changed me. It's made me realise how lucky I am that I come from a wealthy country: the society we have, the freedom we have, the lifestyle we have, the temperature we have. And in the world according to Frazer, I'm luckiest of all that I have a lovely wife and two beautiful children, Charlotte and Freddy.

COLOUR SERGEANT WAYNE HARROD

'Good in the jungle . . .'

I like Brunei because it's proper jungle. When you're abseiling into the jungle from a Bell 212 helicopter and getting a view from above the trees, it looks just like broccoli below and goes on for miles and miles and miles. The scale of the jungle can be daunting. There is a tiny landing pad underneath your feet and if you miss the pad, it would take them two, maybe three days to find your body.

First thing about living in the jungle is coming to terms with the climate. It's very hot and humid and the heat doesn't drop at night, nor does the humidity, so you're even dehydrating at night. Water is your saviour in the jungle and every time you're near a water source you must take on an extra two or three litres, which you can carry inside your bergen. Obviously you've got to purify the water because of all the bacteria, so you drop a couple of Puritabs into your bottle, wait fifteen minutes and they'll kill off all of the bacteria. They give the water a slight chlorine taste and after drinking purified water for a while, you can smell

167

it coming out of your pores – it smells bloody horrible, like ammonia.

You learn about the fauna and flora inside the jungle: you have to know what you can and can't touch, which plants you can eat and which plants have barbs on them, and about the different tree formations. Your big trees have big buttress roots and mangrove swamps have trees that are heavily rooted too. They're very hard going, particularly as you can be in over your waist in water, so you can't see your footing. You have to learn about all the insects and what hazards are inside the rivers. The main poisonous things to look out for are snakes, but as long as you don't start harassing them you'll be fine – they'll just observe and watch. You get some scorpions inside the trees, but they generally don't attack – it's just if you get in their way they'll give you a quick nip.

Even in the daytime you're not talking about a lot of visibility inside a primary jungle. You can only see for about twenty-five metres. The furthest you ever go on patrol before you halt is three hundred metres: you hold patrol, quick nav check, make sure you're going on the right bearing and then it's off again. Everybody's got little tachographs, which are flicked every ten metres. Nevertheless, one day we were patrolling through the trees and started along what looked like a bog-standard track, until suddenly the trees opened up and we realised we were walking on top of a massive log. It must have been at least five foot across. It had fallen over a ravine. We looked down and below us was a thirty- or forty-metre drop. That was an awe-inspiring moment.

It's so dark at night you can't see the hand in front of your face, let alone the moon or the stars. As soon as you start wandering off, that's it, you're lost, so movement is minimal at night. In the jungle you pair up and the most important thing is to look after your buddy, keep an eye on him and make sure he is fit and well. Inside your hide, everything is an arm's distance from you and you're living in close proximity with each other. You get quite a few leeches in the jungle, so you check each other for leeches or ticks and if he's got any problems, you help sort them out. Because of the damp and wet conditions inside the trees, you can get quite bad blisters, plus foot rot and crotch rot. Your fingers become all clammy and horrible; you develop quite a few sores underneath your arms and shoulders; and tropical ulcers just seem to bubble up all over the place.

Any longer than two weeks in that environment and your body starts to degrade and rot – for one thing, it hasn't had the right vitamins because you've been on rations for two weeks. You live off river yams and ginger and there's a particular tree that has very tough and aggressive bark but has a pith which tastes something like cabbage. You'll also be eating little river fish and shrimp – you just make a small fire and cook them as normal, but they're very thin, so you need a lot of them. Maybe you'll find fresh fruit in the jungle, but you can't go round picking or hacking vegetation because that would give away your position.

As it is a dirty place, you have to have discipline. Any letting-up of personal discipline would be the biggest danger. For example, you've got day combats and night combats. Your day combats will be completely soaked with dirt, sweat, camouflage cream and insect repellent, but your night-time combats should be dry and fresh, so as soon as you've changed into your dry

169

combats you're straight into bed. You get changed back into the wet clothing in the morning. If you get that wrong one night, or your personal admin slacked a bit and you couldn't be bothered to change back into your wet combats, that could be the beginning of the end. You are physically very tired inside the trees, but if there's just one non-thinking moment, if you didn't look after your body, and didn't look after the way you were eating, or if you didn't purify your water, that's the thing that will bite you. It wouldn't take long before you'd get sucked into the jungle, and you'd be dead.

It's a good hard environment to work in, but you've got to be self-disciplined in the most hostile territory. It's a good soldier who is good in the jungle and I think jungle training has made all of us better individual soldiers than we would otherwise have been.

CAPTAIN TIM ILLINGWORTH

'This was one of those stories where if you were to write a logical ending, it was not going to be a happy one . . .'

I was put forward by my unit for a trawl to Afghanistan on the initial Herrick deployment to Helmand in 2006. There was no job description laid down for what we were expected to do. We were told initially that we were going to be working with the Afghan Army who were going to come out of the military training centre in Kabul. We'd do on-the-job training and then send them off on operations. But the day before we were due to go, we were told we were going to deploy with them on the ground and do operational stuff alongside them. We were slightly concerned as this hadn't been resourced in terms of the equipment we would need to do the job. We didn't have any vehicles, no support weapons, GPMGs or under-slung grenade launchers. All we had was our personal weapons. It didn't work out that badly, however, because when we got to Helmand, the Afghans we were

171

supposed to be mentoring hadn't finished training, so we had a bit of time to gather some kit together.

I went to watch these guys pass off at their end-of-course parade, which was a very interesting experience. The Afghans are ethnically diverse and it was strange seeing an army of completely different-looking people. The guys from the north-east look Chinese and totally different from the guys from the north-west, who look Mongolian. And you get people who look like Russians or Pakistanis too. Plus, they all have different cultures and some-times different languages.

The Afghans were very proud to be joining the Afghan Army, but they had had twelve weeks from street to soldier, which is not dissimilar to what we do with our guys, but with ours we have very robust training regimes that they don't necessarily have. Also, they passed out as a battalion of five hundred all at the same time, so there was zero experience across the ranks, which seemed very strange to us because we get recruits coming in from training and drip feed them in as natural wastage goes through – so you've always got a level of experience in a battalion.

They went into an Afghan camp in Kandahar where they were issued with all their kit. They had been given somewhere in the region of fifty brand-new American Ford Ranger pick-up trucks, all painted brown with the Afghan Army logo on the bonnet. They loved them; they thought Christmas had come early, although half had never driven a vehicle before and hadn't a clue how to use them.

Not all the guys who had passed their training turned up in Kandahar. Some of them went on permanent holiday. Also, after they had been issued with kit, some of the guys just jumped over the fence and went home, 'Thanks very much, not for me . . .' because there was no real enforcement or discipline in the new unit at the time, and to a certain extent in Afghan culture. Everything's *inshallah* or 'God willing'. We were supposed to have a battalion of five hundred, but we ended up with about two hundred Afghans and we basically accelerated the move, to get them straight down to Camp Bastion as they were never going to jump over the fence there, because it would take a three-week walk through the desert to get to wherever they wanted to go.

We then began to do a lot of training. Initially a lot of the officers' attitude was 'We don't do work', and you very rarely saw them doing anything. But certainly, as we went on operations, they started to catch on that officers were very much expected to be at the frontline, commanding their troops – mainly because those who were reluctant were being dragged along by a British counterpart who was saying, 'What are you going to do now?' 'You should tell your guys to do this . . .' which was all part of the mentoring process.

We took these Afghan guys and went up to a place called FOB (Forward Operating Base) Robinson, south of Sangin, and took over the camp, which was very sparse. The Americans had moved out and ripped everything out and taken it with them, so there weren't any beds or furniture. It was quite literally Hesco bastion and that was it. We spent the first month of the tour under ponchos and a roll mat on the floor trying to keep the dust off, which was great because it kind of set the tone: if you are living in that sort of environment, you are very aware you are on operations.

Shortly after arriving, we were trold that the town was full of Taliban and were ordered to 'seize Sangin'. We weren't quite convinced that our Afghan Army counterparts would be up for this – or up to it – but we went in anyway, had no trouble and had a really good look round Sangin. We had interpreters with us and would go out on patrol and touch base with the local people to find out what was going on in the town.

Our commander then said, 'I want to send a small team to live with the district chief.' I went with three Brits and five Afghans, and we lived in his house, right in the centre of Sangin. The chief welcomed us initially, but he started getting a little bit colder the longer we stayed, probably because we weren't really providing anything for him. His militia were constantly around, high on drugs, so we slept in a room very much with pistols loaded, and one out of four of us on sentry all the time. A few days after this, a platoon of Royal Irish moved into the building next door, which gave us some security, so we were relatively happy.

My team was struck down with stomach troubles and was replaced by another, but then things started to go quite badly wrong when the district chief was overheard on the phone saying, 'Yes, they haven't really got many weapon systems, so you can come in and take them whenever you want.' To cut a long story short, we had taken sides with a guy who had dubious loyalties and had at various times sided with the Russians and the Taliban. We got slightly concerned and pulled out.

We had one incident towards the end of my time in Sangin. A UAV went down on the far side of the river and one of the patrols was re-tasked to go over and see if they could recover it. Although there was probably never any chance of finding it, this patrol got across the river and spoke to the local people. 'No, not seen it, not seen it,' they were told and they started to come back across the river. Between the river and the canal there were only two crossing points, one right up at the top and the other down at the bottom. The patrol got caught in an ambush and were pinned down in an open area. They took one casualty and were fighting for their position where they could, while the Afghans with them just disappeared off.

So we then mounted everyone available into vehicles to go to try and relieve them. We were struggling to get through to a crossing point and as we dismounted, there was an ambush on our patrol and a good friend of mine, a guy called Captain Jim Philippson, was killed. He was one of the first soldiers killed in Helmand. I saw one of the guys, Steve Jones, who had been stood next to him when he was killed, was very shaken by the whole thing, so I sat him at the back of the vehicle, calmed him down, got somebody to watch him and then went back to try and link up with all the guys forward.

It was chaotic and getting people to make decisions at that point was quite a challenge. We couldn't get across. We still had people out on the ground who were under fire. We had a casualty who we had to evacuate. What do we do now? Where do the priorities lie? We loaded Jim's body into the back of the Humvee – it was the first time I had ever seen someone dead – and drove back up to the camp, dropped him off and went back out again pretty much straight away. It was a difficult night: losing a friend, getting his body laid out, but then having to snap out of it, all within five minutes.

The Afghans said there was no way they were going out again. They knew their limitations. Actually, by and large, we were probably better on our own, without the confusion of having Afghans with us. We went out again with just Brits and tried to get back to our guys.

We managed to get across the canal at the southern crossing point and drove along a sort of canal towpath – we then suddenly came under fire from the far side of the canal. We had another guy injured, in that Sergeant Major Andy Stockton had an RPG quite literally go through his arm, which he lost below the elbow, and it wedged in the door of the vehicle but didn't detonate, which was very lucky because if it had exploded, it would have killed him and probably the driver and top gunner as well.

We eventually got out of the ambush and met up with the patrol that had been cut off. We got a Chinook to come and pick up two casualties and then stayed out there all night. A company of Paras flew in the following morning to walk us out, basically. That was our first major incident and from thereon people started realising it was quite a serious tour and the enemy were out there, because until then there hadn't been a huge amount of actual kinetic action.

I felt pretty depressed at the end of that episode. The whole thing had just been so chaotic, which I fully expected, but I was slightly irritated that we had been forced into that situation, by and large, by the fact that we hadn't got firepower, we hadn't got the kit and the Afghans weren't up to it. But that's just the way it was at that very early stage of operations in Afghanistan.

About a week later, I went on R & R almost slap bang in the middle of my tour. Landing in Brize Norton, I still had dust in my hair, I had got a big beard, and Jules, my fiancée, didn't recognise me when I walked through the door. She was like, 'Oh, wow, it is you,' and she had loads of chatter and did what she does, which is talk all the way through to the hotel. It was great, really good to see her, but it was all very odd. For one thing, after having been sleeping on a dusty camp cot and eating whatever you can cook in a mess tin, staying in a hotel in the middle of Oxfordshire is almost like the shock of capture: 'Oh yeah, that's what running water is. I can drink out of the tap, oh right.' You get used to not having things out there, to being dusty and not being able to shower every day, and not being able to shave at all.

But also, you've just had intense, life-changing experiences in a very difficult environment and seen things that have pretty much completely altered your perception of life and death, and, without sounding too melodramatic, your place in the universe. Then you get back here and everything is just ticking along, and it's quite literally like you have dropped into a different world.

Jules was always saying, 'Oh, we've got to have this done by then' or 'You've got to do the washing up, it's really important.' Eventually I had to sit her down and say, 'You have got to understand my perception of what is important has completely altered. I am not going to get excited if nobody's going to get hurt over it. It just won't register.'

Two weeks isn't long for R & R and all that time I was very much in that other world of Afghanistan. That's what matters because that's life-and-death stuff. I had just one last thing to do before I left. I had missed Jimmy's funeral and Jules came up to St Albans to the cathedral where he is buried, and then left me alone to go and sit by his grave and cry my eyes out, and all that sort of stuff. He was very much a soldier. He had done P

177

Company. He had done the commando course. He was a really good guy.

When I got back to Afghanistan we were working with a group that had come out of training. I was mentoring one of their company commanders, a guy called Daoud. He was a northern Afghan, up from the Panchir Valley, and he was a really good guy, brilliant. We would play chess – he would always beat me – and talk about all sorts of subjects: military things and life in general, me in my poor Dari and Daoud in his better English. I learned such a lot from him and, more importantly, we really got on.

Daoud was a leader, which was actually quite rare for the Afghan Army. He ran his company well and he also had a very good sergeant major and some pretty good officers, and he had instilled a system where they did what he told them. His company would be the only company that was getting things done because the other commanders just didn't have that grip over their men. This made my job a pleasure, so I was really happy with him.

We trained up for a number of weeks and I was then sent to mentor a company based at Lashkar Gah, away from Daoud. I went to Lashkar Gah in command of a team of fourteen Brits, and did a load of patrolling there, working with the Afghan Army guys and also the provincial reconstruction team. We were there for a couple of weeks before Garmsir, which was untouched by the Brits up to that point, gathered momentum. The police down there had been under siege for three months and we were tasked to take some of our Afghans and go and see just what was going on.

We slowly picked our way down there through the desert and sat down with the chief of police from the district centre. We gave him a plan of the town and he went, 'Well, the Taliban have taken over *here*. They have been attacking *this* area all the time. We are constantly fighting, but we are OK. We will keep going.'

'OK,' I said. 'Here's our phone number. If you have any problems give us a call.' He then jumped into his vehicle and came under heavy machine-gun fire on the way back out – but they were just used to it.

We went out into the desert and got into a position to see what was going on to the south of the village where the majority of this fighting was coming from. We found an open area where we could get ourselves into a lay-up and went to sleep for the night on the desert floor by the vehicles. We went back in again the following morning and all hell had broken loose. The chief of police said, 'They have taken over the northern checkpoint during the night. Five of our guys are captive, we've got several guys wounded and we are out of ammunition – we've had enough, we're leaving.' We tried to make them stay, but it was, 'Well, you're here now, *you* can look after it.' He didn't realise we weren't there to take over from him.

Some of our Apache helicopters on station had seen lots of armed people around a certain building and the chief of police said, 'Yes, that's the building they have captured,' so the Apaches blew it up. Three of the guys who had been captured managed to escape when the building was destroyed.

The chief was very grateful. 'But it doesn't change anything,' he said. 'I am still going.' So he went and we started getting mortared ourselves, shells were landing within thirty yards, so we moved behind a big mound and got mortared again – we went up into the high ground four kilometres to the east. A round landed about twenty feet in front of us. We spoke to the headquarters up in Lash and told them what had happened and they told us to head back up north to regroup.

When we got back to Lash we went into a planning cycle with the Afghans to recapture the whole town and try to push the Taliban south. I was dealing with the Afghan Army side of life. A guy called Doug Beattie was dealing with the Afghan police, and Paddy Williams dealt with the overall command and control. Between the three of us we came up with what we were going to do. The Afghan Army said they would provide a hundred men. The Afghan police said they would provide the same, and we had our British team of about seventeen. But we were slightly concerned because this was kinetic war fighting: advance to contact, clear the area, which we weren't really scaled for. We were not a credible fighting force to go into that sort of situation – there was clearly a substantial enemy force there.

The brigade commander asked us what we needed to do the job, so I went away with my sergeant major Tommy Johnston and had a long hard think about it. We came back with a wish list, you know, like a kiddie's wish list if you were told at Christmas that you could have anything you wanted, write what you want. So we basically did that. 'We want another WMIK, we want .50 calibre machine guns, we want this and we want that . . .' Went back to the brigade commander and he said, 'Right, call my supply guy at the brigade. He is expecting your call.'

I rang this guy and he said, 'Yes, OK, fine. You can have all that and I also suggest you take this and that and the other, and

I'll have them over to you today.' Some of the things he mentioned I didn't even know existed, but the effort they were going to to get us the kit gave me the feeling that we were doing a serious job. Everyone out there knew what we were going out to do, so they were incredibly supportive. Take what rations you like. Take new boots. Oh, and empty out the ammunition store. We'll give you everything you need. I went back to my sergeant major and he asked what they'd said about our wish list and I said, they will have it with us today. He looked at me and said, 'They are actually going to ask us to do this, aren't they?'

'Yes,' I said. 'They are.'

We had been asked to walk into a situation where we knew there were a number of enemy. Seventeen Brits with supposedly two hundred Afghans, going down to do a war-fighting job, recapturing a district . . . This was one of those stories where if you were to write a logical ending, it was not going to be a happy one. And it was within two weeks of our end of tour. We had been there for five and a half months and most of the guys on my team had been caught up in the incident at Sangin, so everyone was on edge

I sat down with all my guys and said, 'Right, this is what we are being asked to do. This will probably be the only chance in your life you will get to do something like this. If anyone doesn't want to do it, I completely understand. Just come and see me and you won't have to go.' I had one young private who had been pretty shaken the first time we went down, and he said, 'This is so far above me, I just can't do it.' So he stayed behind and I put somebody in to replace him – there is no shortage of complete lunatics who want to go on a trip like this. My British team was made up of all sorts: Royal Logistic Corps, Army Air Corps, Royal Signals. Out of the seventeen, only four of us were infantry, i.e. guys for whom this was our normal job. And those four weren't from my regiment – they were from all different places, but we were really close at that particular point.

I was half nervous and half excited. It was a very exciting challenge. There are only so many times that you as an infantryman get to do your job and I am probably one of the very few who have had to do it under those circumstances – although I wasn't commanding regular infanteers, I was commanding a mish-mash of all sorts of people, who were, in turn, mentoring Afghans.

Paddy, myself and Doug delivered orders to all the guys to make sure everyone knew exactly what we were doing. Because it was a fairly large operation we had a map up on the board of the route we were going to take, all the times and detail of what was going to happen, actions on vehicles breaking down, where we were going to break in, and how we were going to split it up in order to clear through the ground we needed to. We had to start a long way north in order to clear the area from the northern crossing point down; basically, to push the enemy far enough south so that their mortars and rockets weren't at liberty to fire into the town, although at the time it was deserted – all the people had just locked up their shops and gone. At this stage the Afghan police and army were gathering together their forces ready to go south. On 10 September we were ready to go.

We had a convoy of two hundred people in vehicles and spent a day travelling down, and we had Afghans breaking down who had to leave their vehicles behind because they just couldn't make it.

As we were heading down, I found to my surprise and joy that Daoud had turned up. I was over the moon to see him. He was all smiles and happy and keen to get on with it. I now had somebody to whom I could say, 'We need to do this,' and he would turn round to his guys and it would happen. Mohammed Kareem, who was the overall commander of the Afghan Army, was pretty useless. Well, maybe that's a bit harsh. Let's say his style of leadership was very Afghan: it was one of rule by debate and if the soldiers didn't want to do something, he wouldn't make them, which makes things difficult when you are trying to get people to walk into the face of the enemy. Nobody in their right mind wants to do that, least of all a seventeen-year-old Afghan who has only done twelve weeks of training.

The plan was the Afghan police would secure the initial crossing point. The Afghan Army would then break through and clear the top area. We would shake out with the Afghan Army on the right-hand side, and the Afghan police on the left-hand side, and then clear the way down and try to recapture the town. Very simple plan and very clear – it had to be simple for all the Afghans to understand it. We lay up in the desert overnight waiting for the following morning.

H-Hour was 0500 on 11 September.

And by and large, but with a few variations, everything went to plan. We went and cleared the crossing point, which took a lot of fighting because the Taliban had trenches. There were a couple of Afghan casualties at that point, one killed and one wounded, shot in the leg. Eventually we managed to break into what was farmland interspersed with buildings. We fought all the way across, clearing the top area so we could then swing round and be ready to push south. The fighting was intense to start with. It took about five hours to capture the main crossing point and probably another two to three hours to get the thousand yards across the canal. By the time we started pushing south, it was fairly clear going, with just a few pockets of resistance here and there.

At the start it wasn't easy. I was in a ditch and there was open ground with bullets flying all over the place, but I needed to get forward to see what the ground was like, and Doug was already across it on his own with the Afghan police. This was the first time I had to deliberately put myself in a position where I knew rounds were coming at me. It was like deciding to dive into a pond of dark water where you're not sure what's under the surface but you are going to have to go in. I ran across the open ground and I could hear the whizz and splash of rounds cutting the air around me and as I joined Doug at the top there were enemy across the far side of the canal, so I engaged them and then pulled myself back and had a look at the situation. That was when Doug and I decided, right, we have cleared this side of the canal, let's go round and capture the northern crossing point.

I went on foot with Mohammed Kareem and made sure he was directing people, and things were going OK. The Afghans were taking casualties, but by and large at that stage they weren't too bad. We got through and started pushing south, and it went smoothly. The Taliban had put lots of people up at the northern crossing points in the area around there, but they hadn't built up any defences in the area they hadn't held before. After we had broken through, they retreated and we cleared the town at about seven or eight o'clock that evening. We had spent thirteen hours fighting and managed to clear and recapture the town, and we had the police back in the police HQ. As first days go, it was pretty successful.

We set out sentry positions to make sure we weren't going to come under attack that night. A few rockets and some mortars came in, missed and exploded wherever, but that first night was pretty quiet. I was shattered but I was happy that things had gone as well as they had. I put a mat on the ground at the back tyre of the vehicle and slept like a log.

The Afghan police were over the moon to be back in their HQ and at that point they decided, 'Job done, we have got the town back.' Whereas our thought was, You haven't got the town back until people are free to move back into it, so you have to push the Taliban further south. We had a line drawn on the map that we needed to clear down to. That's when it started getting really tricky telling the Afghans, 'No, it's not done, we need to push on south.' Certainly the Afghan Army couldn't quite see why.

We had a few cups of *chai* with the chief of police and Mohammed Kareem and changed his mind. The next day we carried on with the plan. The Afghan police were pretty effective under Doug and made good ground, but the Afghan Army I was with very quickly ran into some stiff resistance. One of the Afghan platoon commanders was shot quite badly in the shoulder. Immediately, they said they weren't cracking on. One guy was being particularly wet. He just wouldn't commit to clearing that ground and kept saying, 'Why do we need to do this? We have this big fort up here. We can seal this ground.' And after one of their commanders had been shot, and they lost another

185

guy, killed, and another two guys, injured, they just went, 'No, that's enough. We'll go back to the fort and fight from there.'

I was really frustrated and Doug was saying, 'What the hell are you doing? We are cracking on and now our right flank is exposed.' I was aware of that. I said to Paddy, 'I can't persuade them to move, so I'll take some I know I can get to come, and go down to Doug and provide some cover for his right flank.' I got Daoud, and about twenty-five to thirty of his guys, and went to the eastern side that Doug was clearing and pushed down to support him. That night we got to a crossing point in the canal on the eastern side. We got the Afghan police manning the crossing point and then Daoud and his guys holed up in a compound and we left them there for the night.

The following morning I picked up some more Afghans and told Mohammed Kareem that these guys were coming with me and that we would be clearing the ground we didn't clear the day before. And that's what we did. We cleared all of the buildings from where we had stopped the previous day, all the way down back to where Daoud was. It was fairly slim resistance until I met up with Daoud, and at that stage Doug had got himself into a contact in an open field where one of our guys had been shot, although fortunately he wasn't too bad. I pushed up to support him with Daoud and set up a static firing point in a deserted compound, engaging the position they were coming under fire from, which then allowed them to withdraw.

We had to clear that area, so we called in some air, but all that was available was a couple of French Mirages, who used small arms weapons to fire into the wood line, but it didn't really do a huge amount. We knew we had to go in anyway, as that wood line and the compound in it were pretty much the final objective and sat just about on the line we had drawn on our map.

I sat down with Daoud in the building we were fighting from. There was probably a gap of a hundred and fifty metres between that building and the building the enemy were in. To the right-hand side was a maize field with about a six-foot-high crop. There was a track running down the middle of the field and on the left-hand side it was fairly open ground. We came up with a plan that we would cut through one of the ditches in the maize field, stay low, get into the ditch at the far side, get shaken out, then push forward the last forty metres and capture the building. We would then have a strong point to fight from to clear the wood line. Daoud was happy with that plan, as was Hammadudin, the other company commander.

When the second air strike went in, we moved out using the cover of the maize field. We got into position and just as we started shaking out, we came under heavy machine gun fire and rocket attack, which made most of the Afghans freeze and hunker down, while Daoud tried to drag people forward, so we would have people there who could fire back. Most of them went, 'No way am I walking into that.' We had one RPG come in about ten to fifteen feet to my right-hand side. It exploded between two of the Afghans, giving them severe shrapnel injuries. Then another one came in and narrowly missed my foot, but for some reason didn't detonate, it skimmed the ground, ricocheted off and detonated in mid-air somewhere just behind Tommy who was about sixty metres behind me, bringing up the Afghans at the rear. That was the point when I thought, Well, if I am going to die, this is probably the time.

It was a case of myself and Daoud trying to get the guys to move forwards into a position that was facing the enemy. But it was all going a bit wrong. We got them there, but they weren't doing what I was doing, which was the typical British Army thing of kneel up, take aim, fire a few rounds, identify targets, get back down again, move, get up. The Afghans were all lying down, occasionally lifting up their AKs and just spraying round in the general direction of the enemy. So Daoud grabbed one of the rocket launchers and I went with him and two other Afghans and we pushed forward in the direction of the enemy. We got to a position where we were able to provide some decent firing on to the enemy. Daoud loaded the rocket launcher, prepped it, knelt up, took aim – and took a round straight through his chest. About forty-five seconds later he was dead, which was not a great turn of events.

At that point the two guys who were with us just burst into tears and literally started the whole Afghan wailing thing, lamenting their lost commander. I carried on firing at the enemy, while they dragged Daoud about ten feet back to the rest of the troops and then I got Hammadudin, who was the only commander alive, and explained to him what I expected, which was to provide more fire, and at the same time to have people take Daoud's body back through the way we had come.

I picked up the rocket launcher Daoud had used, plus the rounds he'd had with him, pushed forwards, prepped it, knelt up, went to fire – and it didn't fire. I had never used one of these things properly. I realised there was a little notch, knelt up again, went to fire, and the safety catch was on, which was slightly disconcerting. Finally, I flipped the switch and fired three

188

rounds into the building and the wood next to it. The first one went high and the other two went into the building. I then put the rocket launcher down and carried on with my rifle, pushed a little bit further forwards and carried on firing at the shadows shooting at us from the woods and building. I ran out of rounds, went to change my magazine and heard absolute silence, and thought, Crap, we are not firing – but neither are they. There was nobody there – they had all gone.

Within seconds the enemy started firing again, at which point I ducked back over a track into the field we had come through – and found Daoud's body with one Afghan sat next to it, crying. By this stage there was fire coming into us because they could probably see the maize moving, but I had to try and get this Afghan to help me drag Daoud's body back to the building we had started from. I couldn't just leave him. Aside from this one man, his guys had all left him, but I'm not leaving him. I thought, If I can get him back, I will. I got this Afghan to take one foot while I took the other and we started to drag him back. We managed about five feet, but the rounds were coming in and eventually – I think one round must have got quite close – this poor Afghan snapped and legged it, leaving me trying to tug Daoud along by both feet. I got him into the field a fair way by lying on my back with his feet in my hands, moving along inch by inch, but by that stage I was absolutely knackered and after a while I couldn't get him any further. Also, the enemy fire was zeroing in on the moving corn and getting a little bit more intense. It became very apparent that (a) there was nobody between me and a lot of very angry people, (b) I was pretty much out of ammunition and (c) actually, he was dead and wasn't going to get any deader.

I lay there for a bit, agonising over leaving him, but when I'd made probably the hardest decision of my life to leave him, I crawled, then scrambled, and then ran as fast as I could to get back to the building where all the Afghans were with Tommy, the sergeant major. He was convinced I had been killed, so when I tipped up he was quite happy, so happy he almost knocked me over with his embrace. Hammadudin immediately came up and said, 'Where's his body? What have you done with Daoud's body?' At which point I slightly lost my temper, and Tommy was fairly forthright, but stopped me from doing anything I shouldn't have done.

I was really upset that Daoud had been killed. I headed back to where Doug's team was and was looking at putting another team together to go back and get the body, but Doug turned round and said, 'No, you are not doing it. If the Afghans want him badly enough, they can do it themselves.' So I sat down with Kareem and drew him a map, and said, 'This is where he is and this is how to get to him without being seen.' Mohammed Kareem then took a team and went in to try and recover the body. Tommy loaded me into the wagon and took me back to the village to get some water and food because by now I was shattered.

The Afghans came back in all sorts of disrepair, but, thankfully, with Daoud's body. They had walked straight across the open field and been engaged with rockets. They had five very seriously injured, with missing feet and body parts. We spent the rest of that night trying to keep these guys alive and got them CASEVACed back to Bastion by helicopter. We cracked on the next couple of days without them. But by that stage getting the Afghan Army to do anything was pretty much impossible. I tried to move them forward, but they just weren't having it. We eventually managed to get them into a building further south out on the western side that dominated the main route up and down. We reinforced it, doing a lot of building up of positions, putting sangars in, barbed wire out, blocking the roads, all that sort of stuff.

And that was it really. All in all, about seven days of fighting. It was all just one big long nightmare.

I had guys who were due to fly back to the UK in three days' time because it was their end of tour, and we were still stuck down in Garmsir. But early the following morning, we left Doug and Paddy holding the fort with the Afghans and headed back to Lash to hand over to the Marines. We spent the next day and a half briefing them up on the situation and all the lessons learned, who the key characters were and what the situation was on the ground.

We flew back to Bastion to get our flights to the UK at the end of the tour and by the time we got to Bastion, I heard that the Marines were having a rough time and couldn't get the Afghans to push any further forwards. This was not great news, and already one of their staff sergeants was in the hospital because he had been shot in the leg. It was a pretty difficult way to leave things.

For a long time I blamed myself that Daoud was killed. If I had been more sensible, I would have guarded him more closely because he was the key to my Afghan success. I was really upset that the Afghans had basically abandoned us. That really got to me. They are a very mixed bunch. Some of them, like Daoud, were very good and very brave, but some of them just move with the flow. If something is working they will go with it, but they won't try and change something that isn't working – it is too much effort. If it is too much like hard work, then it's *inshallah*, it's God's will.

But, by and large, the ones who were with me were a group of young men who had had twelve weeks of training and had then been sent on a war-fighting mission to recapture a district, so I have no problems with them whatsoever.

Official citation accompanying Conspicuous Gallantry Cross for Acting Captain Timothy Illingworth, Light Infantry

On 10 September 2006, Lieutenant Timothy Illingworth deployed with a small team in support of a joint Afghan Police and Army operation to recapture Garmsir District Centre. During two days of heavy fighting, Lieutenant Illingworth and his team were constantly under fire whilst motivating, directing and advising their Afghan colleagues who successfully re-took Garmsir. Later that week an Afghan Police patrol supported by Illingworth's team, was ambushed. One British casualty resulted. In an effort to relieve the pressure on the Afghan Police, he led his Afghan company commander and a foot patrol to neutralise the enemy position. This inspired his Afghan Army colleagues who were reticent to advance on the heavily defended enemy position.

The Afghani resolve to continue failed after three days of heavy fighting. Seeing this, Lieutenant Illingworth went to the front of the Afghan troops and moved alone to within 30 metres of the first enemy position under heavy fire. Soon after the company commander was killed. Lieutenant Illingworth took up the commander's rocket launcher, firing three rounds into the main enemy position in full view of them. He himself narrowly missed being killed. All but one of the Afghan force abandoned Illingworth, leaving him exposed and under withering fire. In spite of his isolation, he attempted to assault the enemy position expending seven magazines of ammunition. The enemy fire was unrelenting. He regrouped and rallied the remaining force to continue.

Lieutenant Illingworth's bravery and example over seven days was well beyond the call of duty. His role was to mentor rather than fight. However, understanding the importance of Garmsir, he placed himself in a position of utmost danger to influence events. His outstanding courage, leadership and selflessness in pressing home his attack upset the enemy ambush and saved many lives. Such inspiring and raw courage from a relatively young and inexperienced officer was exemplary and justly merits the award of the Conspicuous Gallantry Cross.

LIEUTENANT COLONEL ANDREW JACKSON

'It's about being a paratrooper . . .'

I had my moments growing up when I was quite out of control. I see my life could have gone a very different way. People who knew me when I was a lot younger say, 'I can't believe you're in the Army and you thrive on that sort of discipline. You always had the tendency to be quite wild.' But people outside the Army don't understand what the Army is all about, particularly as an officer. Yes, it has a firm structure, but the leeway and the latitude and the level of responsibility I have, particularly on operations in charge of soldiers, is incredible, far more than you'd ever get in a civilian job. The Army's very good at believing the more trust you place in someone, the more they will live up to it.

But I've always believed joining the Army is quite Faustian, in that it's a good career, there's a good pension, it's exciting stuff, lots of sports, adventuring, good exercise, good fun and good comradeship; but you're not being paid for what you can do, you're being paid for what you might have to do, and the fact is

194

that there's always a possibility you might have to kill, and put your own life at risk, going on operations, doing difficult things.

For me, it's not about being a soldier, it's about being a paratrooper. In my mind, the Parachute Regiment is the embodiment of what soldiering is about. The Parachute Regiment's soldiers are just awesome, and the privilege of commanding paratroopers as an officer in the Parachute Regiment is fantastic.

The operation that made the single biggest impression on me wasn't one where I was out on the ground, it was one where I was running things from the ops room in Sangin. Don't imagine Star Trek Command, think the other end of the technological spectrum: an old building that had been built up with sandbags and a bit of engineer roofing to protect it from shells and mortar fire.

We were mounting an air assault operation up into the north of our valley. It was accepted that there was probably some enemy up there and we needed to go and see what the lie of the land was, but it wasn't intended to be all-out fighting; ideally it needed to be non-offensive and probing. In the event, there were more enemy forces on the ground than expected and they reacted very fast to our force's arrival. Casualties were taken and the tempo of the operation ramped up almost instantaneously. Simultaneously, unusual things started to happen further down the valley from us, where the battalion had a number of other more routine, day-to-day taskings – what we call 'framework ops' – going on. Very quickly, an extremely complex and confusing overall scenario built up. Factors such as our own casualties, possible civilian casualties, poor radio comms, misunderstandings with our Afghan Army counterparts and so on, all suddenly came together at once to create the highest risk and most potentially dangerous battle picture we had had to contend with up to that point in our tour. The overall situation was in danger of running out of control as my team struggled to cope with this 'sensory overload'. Our position was further exacerbated by having a number of key individuals 'out of action' thanks to a particularly virulent D & V bug – both on the ground and back in the ops room. It was the same sort of scenario that they conjure up in a training exercise, where they deliberately pile on the complexities and the confusion and the layers to see where your breaking point is, although if they had thrown that much simultaneous activity and coincidental distractions into one exercise scenario during our pre-deployment training, I would not have thought it was realistic or have believed that it would ever get that bad for real.

Now, in the event, we got the helicopters back in after twenty-four hours to extract our air assault forces and all the other peripheral problems were successfully taken care of, but there were a number of casualties taken during that operation and a lot of soul-searching by those who had planned and executed it as to whether it had been done the right way – you always ask yourself if you could have avoided these things.

In many ways, once you've planned something and put your heart and soul into it – once you've asked soldiers to go and do it, and they've looked you in the eye and you've looked them in the eye – when things go wrong it becomes personal. I don't think we could have done anything any differently, but it still goes through your head. The most important thing after any operation is what we call an after-action review: you go over

The thing that really irks me when I come back to the UK is the way people drive, and the road rage. You'll be in a car with your children and someone – Mr X, who is account manager at Mole Valley Valves and is five minutes late for his production meeting at Trudge Mill – will pull off some stunt that is liable to cause an RTA. And you think, I can't believe I've been through six months of Afghanistan, where I looked after myself very well, thank you very much, and come back here and have you take risks with my life and the lives of my family.

I was second in command of 2 PARA in Afghanistan last summer. Then I was lucky enough to pick up a promotion, so I came back to the UK to command the 2nd Infantry Training Battalion, which is really good news for me as I had a really bad parachute accident a few years ago and broke my back and I can't jump any more.

We were testing jumping from a new model of the C-130 Hercules. As is normal for Paras, we jumped from six hundred feet, which gives you between nine and twelve seconds in the air, so if your chute fails to open correctly, as mine did – or didn't – you have a minimum amount of time to try and work out what you are going to do about it. The Parachute School's official motto is 'Knowledge Dispels Fear', i.e. the more you know about a problem, the less it should scare you, which the soldiers invert to 'Fear Dispels Knowledge' because the more frightened you are, the less you can remember anything you've bloody well been told.

In this instance, as soon as I got out of the plane I knew there was a twist in the canopy and I was trying to open it up, but couldn't. I had to decide whether to pull my reserve or not.

In training they tell you to pull your reserve if you've got half a main chute. But you always worry that a reserve parachute could entangle with it and then you're probably stuffed anyway. It appeared to be sorting itself out, so I decided not to deploy the reserve and go with what I had.

We have a great saying in the Parachute Regiment: 'A parachute has no reverse gear.' The reason we train guys the way we do is that once you step into the unknown, you're off, and when things don't go as you expect them to, you've got to make them work and live with the consequences, which is a good maxim for life, isn't it? We also have another great saying in parachuting: 'If you leave the aircraft and something goes wrong with your parachute, do not panic, you have the rest of your life to sort out the problem . . .'

I could see the ambulance driving towards where I was coming down. They had obviously seen me coming down faster than everybody else – and when you see the medics hammering towards your predicted point of impact, it's never a thing calculated to fill you with much optimism. I hit the deck very hard and got a compound compression fracture in my vertebrae. There's a lot of us who jump who have had bad injuries, and the truth is, when you load up an aircraft to go on a jump, you know damn well, by the law of averages, someone's going to have a bad landing and going to get injured. That's why it's such good preparations for operations.

Military parachuting is a fairly miserable, dangerous and unpleasant experience from start to finish. You wait around for hours. You usually get to do it in the middle of the night, and you're messed around from pillar to post by the RAF as a sort of living freight. I know there's a good reason for that. It's a compli-cated activity. There're lots of checks to be done and the loading is precise – it takes time. The RAF do it in a controlled, hands-on manner and, to be fair, they're very good at it. As a contrast, we went parachuting out of a helicopter with the German Air Force, just half a dozen jumpers and a German jump-master, and it was all a bit chaotic, like a bunch of blokes on the piss, getting out of a taxi, by the cashpoint, on a Saturday night.

The Royal Marines have always had primacy in Arctic warfare, but with an Army battalion to reinforce them. The Paras took on the role. We were the last Army organisation to do it before the retraction of the Russian threat and cash considerations meant that the Marines took it on in its entirety.

The battalion did it in true Parachute Regiment tradition. We fired into it with bags of enthusiasm and not a whole load of consideration of the problems; we're a cross-that-bridge-when-we-come-to-it organisation.

Of course, the Norwegians with whom we were doing exer-cises had been skiing since they were children. Their soldiers were skiing downhill like something out of a James Bond movie: no sticks, weapons at the ready, leaping over moguls, just moving perfectly and tactically. Then we'd be like the Keystone Cops: people falling over and bumping into each other, and when it got to the line of departure, everyone would stack into everyone else. It was just farcical really. Thank God, we never fought for real out there.

A lot is always made of the skills you need to fight in the jungle, but ultimately, jungles are pretty benign, i.e. you could put your bergen down in a clearing and sit there for twenty-four hours and you would still be there – although obviously you have to watch out for things that can bite you. The Arctic will kill you in a heartbeat if you are not equipped for it, so you have to put an awful lot of energy into surviving before you can even think about fighting – 90 per cent of fighting in the Arctic is surviving the Arctic. I always thought that at the micro-tactical level, the term 'Arctic warfare' was a bit incongruous because the landscape channels you to such a huge degree, and it takes so much to survive, that your ability to conduct meaningful combat is pretty limited.

The preparation for getting into and out of your tent is just laborious in the extreme. Before you get into the tent, you have to make sure that everyone gets all the snow off them, so they're not bringing in water. If you go out of your tent, you've got to put your fleece boots on. You have to be absolutely religious about your procedures and looking after your kit. Everyone's clothes have to come off and be dried, so you take off your socks and put them under your armpits to dry out at night. Your boots go inside your bivi bag, or they would be absolutely rock solid by the morning. You have to keep rifles outside because they would rust if you brought them into the tent. Every man gets issued four water bottles and those who are intelligent get themselves an extra bottle, mark it brightly and appropriately, and use it as a piss bottle that you keep in your sleeping bag at night – and you make damn sure your aim is good . . .

There's always a tent rhino, The tent rhino is that individual who can be relied upon to bring snow into the tent or knock the light or stove over, or set fire to your sleeping bag. You know, 'Oops, 'scuse I, oh sorry, sorry, only me . . .' About two days into a week-long ski patrol, we had someone knock the stove over, it burnt through my inflatable roll mat and I couldn't repair it. The remaining days I was absolutely gibbering every night because I was so freezing cold.

There are people who really struggle in the Arctic and there are others who thrive in it and become extremely good soldiers out there. It's a shame that the Army doesn't have that much to do with it any more because it is a really good and different experience.

CAPTAIN TOM KELLY
'It's a lottery...'

I am privileged to have seen pretty much all of Afghanistan. I have been all the way from Kabul down to Helmand and across the north-east through the desert and it's unspoilt, fantastic landscape. The rolling deserts of the north that go up towards Tajikistan and Turkmenistan are absolutely stunning and when the sun hits them, it turns the sand into a glorious, lustrous red. I have driven across the Hindu Kush in the snow and watched the sun crest across the top, and seen the early morning mist whispering across the Green Zone, which is so beautiful – and it looks just like Britain, which is the biggest shock.

My first tour of Afghanistan was a benign tour to do with security-sector reform for the country's north-west provinces, an area which is very much based on a feudal system. There were six of us working in a province the size of Wales and the only way you could do it was through engaging with people on a personal level, where there would be a key warlord and several lower warlords. These warlords are savvy men, who have been around the block. They have fought battles in the Soviet war, they've fought the Taliban and some of them have changed sides on several occasions and know to support the side that is going to win.

The hospitality codes are extremely important to the Afghans. You would arrive at a place and the warlord would treat you as if you were brothers: big hug – he'd probably kiss you on several occasions – which was always hilarious to the rest of my troops sat in their vehicles. Next a big handshake and they would hold your hand, I mean really grip it, and that was it – you'd be holding hands for twenty, twenty-five minutes. The fellas loved watching me having to walk around like that. I would then be taken to a meeting where I'd sit at the head of the room with the warlord himself and all of his minor commanders. This was his basic show of force and you would then have an exchange of pleasantries in the very basic Dari all of us commanders had learned.

There is a lot of highly active equipment left over from the Soviet era that could be used at any time to restart a conflict. I would go to a place and say, 'Have you handed in all your weapons?'

'Yes,' they would reply.

'Absolutely all your weapons?' I would say. 'No AK47s?'

They would sit there with grins on their faces and repeat, 'We have got absolutely nothing,' while having a guard stood right behind me with an AK47.

'What about that one?' I'd ask.

'OK, we have got one AK47.'

It was like, '*You* find the rest then,' which I found amusing because they are such personable people.

There would inevitably be an invite to stay for dinner. That was always an interesting challenge. First came the bread, which had been kneaded by somebody's feet, and then the main course would come out in a giant vat. People would look at me and say, 'Please, you are the guest, you are first.' There were no knives and forks, you had to delve in with your hand and grab whatever was floating around in there – generally non-disclosed bits of meat. You could be eating chopped up lamb or goat, or God knows what, and everyone is watching you as it goes into your mouth. Most of it was tasty, however, every now and again some of it would turn you inside out. It was a lottery. I would invite different people on my team to come in with me to sample a dinner, but after they had been through it once, it was always, 'No, you're going on your own, mate.'

My second tour in Afghanistan was entirely different. On one occasion we had been driving down the Salang highway that links the entirety of Afghanistan and the Taliban appeared to have been tracking us for quite a long period of time. They didn't engage until about two o'clock in the afternoon. We were hit from our flank, a lot of AK47 fire over our heads, then they started to RPG and mortar us, which was an unbelievable feeling, just completely exhilarating. My goodness, someone has actually decided to have a shot at us! Or was it someone shooting at someone else and had completely missed? It is not uncommon for people in Afghanistan to celebrate events by shooting guns. I know one area where the warlord's wife gave birth to a son and he was so excited that he lined up all his troops and had them fire everything they had across the valley. Unfortunately, across the valley was another clan, who misinterpreted the gunfire, and fired everything back, and the observers were all going, 'Something's kicking off at a huge level.'

At the beginning of that operation, we saw something I shall never forget. The Taliban executed eleven Afghan national police and we found each of them where they'd been killed. That was the first time I'd properly seen dead people. It was pretty horrendous. The fear on their faces was awful to see. The Taliban had shot the first guy through the back of the head, and the rest of them must have thought, Right, we're all going to die, let's get out of here. They started running, but their hands were tied and the Taliban got on motorbikes and tracked after them. Over about four kilometres, we came across these men. Many of them lay curled up in the foetal position. A bullet had been fired into the back of all of their heads. I saw this one bloke with his brains blown out; his eyes had turned into his head and his face was just a big hole, which was pretty disgusting. Only one guy managed to get away. He ran into our patrol while the Taliban were tracking him and he was terrified. That really galvanised my commitment to do as much as I could do to stop the Taliban.

That sort of stuff isn't ever on the news back in the UK, but I don't think the country is ready to see real war. I don't think they should either. It's not particularly nice. It's pretty grim. If people saw the results of operational tours, where we killed several thousand Taliban, which is an incredible amount of people . . . it would be pretty horrendous to see. People just need to know that the lads are fighting tooth and nail every

207

day. I don't think they need to see what actually comes out of that.

I was the mortar fire officer for the regiment. At the start of the tour I made a trip to Garmsir, which is the most southern position we hold in Afghanistan. It was the first time I had ever been into a real combat zone and I went up to JTAC Hill, the only dominating ground within the area. From that position you have pretty much unrivalled arcs to the south of the location. I was looking through my binoculars, and about two kilometres away I saw a coat swinging in a tree. I cross-referenced it with the guys down there and it was an enemy sentry position. We hit it with mortars later on that day. It felt quite incredible that we were standing there, well, for want of a better word, killing the Taliban. It was pure exhilaration, like, 'I'm actually doing the job I was meant to do as an infanteer.' When it does happen, it's like, 'Thank God, that's done,' I can finally say, 'I've been there, done that, come out the other end, and did my job.' Everything has been working towards this point when you can finally say, 'I have fought an enemy.' That's why we all join the Army. Some guys have spent twenty-two years in the Army and never been shot at, never killed someone. They have been like a coiled spring for years, waiting for this to happen.

I think the most mental thing I experienced was being in FOB Arnhem, which is sat on the edge of the Green Zone. I used to go up in the tower every day and it would regularly come under indirect fire from mortars or rockets. Over time they got more and more accurate, and one day they put a rocket right into the position I was stood in. I can remember just standing there shaking, knowing that as I couldn't see their position, I was completely powerless to do anything about it, but unless I could see exactly who was firing, I wasn't willing to risk killing civilians. I can't have that on my conscience. We had the locating radar, which told me roughly where they were, so of course you could fire off like a mad man and shoot rounds all over the place. But that wasn't enough for me. Are you going to hit him? No. Are you doing anything other than making a noise to make the lads feel better? No, you are just being dangerous. So as much as the lads would like to hear the mortars going off every second and be able to say, 'That sounds great, someone must be getting leathered out there,' it would achieve nothing.

It is pretty demoralising if you're not in a position to fire back when someone is smashing you with rockets, with the sole intention of trying to kill you. If that happens on a day-to-day basis for a long period of time, it does begin to wear on you, particularly if you start thinking about the odds: the number of bullets being fired, the number of mines that are out there. You think to yourself, I've been in ten or fifteen big firefights now, the odds are that something is going to get me. It does begin to grate, and if you can't deal with it, it will degrade you as a soldier. It's called freezing in combat.

Unfortunately a lot of people in our regiment were killed on that tour. I was in the ops room when the first guy from our regiment was killed. All that comes over the radio is 'We've got a T4 casualty,' which equates to 'Somebody's been killed', and you get the person's ID, a mixture of numbers and letters. There's so much stuff going on, you can't work out immediately who it might be. Later on, once the contacts have calmed down and things have begun to stabilise, you eventually realise who it is . . . Lance Corporal Paul 'Sandy' Sandford was a private soldier in my platoon when I first joined the regiment, so I'd spent two and a half years with him, and was incredibly fond of him. About two weeks later, Drummer Thomas Wright, who was in my platoon for a similar period of time, was killed, and also Sergeant Craig Brelsford, who was a corporal with me for the entire first Afghan tour. I was very close to him. The same day as Sergeant Brelsford was killed, a big South African fella called Private Johan Botha, a fantastic bloke who I'd trained from the first day he joined the Army, was also killed. He'd just got married and had a kid. It was pretty horrendous stuff, and it really hits you hard.

Unfortunately, on my very last operation in Helmand, Anders, a Danish commander who had looked after me extremely well, was killed in a Taliban attack. He took a piece of shrapnel to his head. We often fought with the Danes and they are terrific soldiers. I always travelled in Anders' vehicle, but by a sheer fluke, this one time I had been sent to another vehicle. The amazing thing is the random factor of war. There's no set rules for death, it just happens. It's a lottery. A guy can be shooting at you and miss with an entire magazine, and then a guy just walking along gets a ricocheted bullet through his head.

It was extremely hard to try and convey our sorrow to the Danes and at the same time maintain a soldierly stiff upper lip. It really stuck in my consciousness that I wasn't able to turn round and say, 'Right, fellas, let's put this right, let's go and find the Taliban that has done this.' It was my last patrol and I didn't have that opportunity. There was a real feeling of unfinished business.

If you've been in a big firefight where someone's been killed, it's best to sit down and assess it through yourself or with the guys around you, so that you can figure things out before you call someone back home and blurt out something that will upset them. In fact, it is best not to phone home at all. You don't get a great deal of time to phone home anyway, and my wife would just worry about me when I did, which put me in a bad way too.

I was privileged to carry the Queen's Colours for two repatriation ceremonies in Camp Bastion. The Queen's Colour and the Regimental Colour had both been flown out to Afghanistan and it was important for me to be able to say one last goodbye. As with any repatriation, it is highly ceremonial; the colour party escort the coffin on to the C-130 with rifles and fixed bayonets. There would be a presentation of arms, then a lowering of the colours as the coffin is carried on to the plane. The flags would be raised as the plane took off, and as it came back over the top, the colours would be lowered again as a mark of respect while the plane dipped its wings in a final salute as it disappeared off to Kandahar.

It is very difficult to switch off when you first come back home. Physically, your commitment has ended, but having been so immersed in it you just can't stop thinking about it. The psychological impact causes your body to react. I came back to England pretty close to Bonfire Night and when a kid threw a firework near to my car, it transported me right back to a firefight. I nearly had a heart attack.

It was extremely important to explain to my wife that quite a lot of stuff had happened. A lot of people had been killed or injured and that had had an impact on me, although I don't want to spend a great deal of time telling my wife because, to be frank, I think it would be a bit unnerving for her. Every man who has to fight has to come terms with killing another human being. She knows I am a soldier. She doesn't really need to know everything it entails.

LIEUTENANT COLONEL NICK KITSON

'One's got to be tough to keep this show on the road ...'

I got back from Afghanistan two days ago. It's always lovely coming back to England, across the green fields, trying to remember what season it was when I left, which was some time in October, so autumn, I reckon. However, nice as it was to be back home, I always have mixed feelings about R & R because it's quite a drain on resources in terms of soldiers available for operations on the front line, where numbers really do matter.

My wife, Kitty, very kindly came down to Brize Norton, all the way from home base in Edinburgh, to welcome me home, but also so we could drive up via Selly Oak and see some of our casualties. We've had eighteen killed in the past three months and many wounded, quite a lot seriously.

I'm the commanding officer of 3 Rifles Battle Group, which is there to provide security in the northern part of Helmand so the Afghan authorities can bed in and economic prosperity can take root. The northernmost extent of our domain is Kajaki, where the dam is; to the south, it's Sangin.

213

Sangin is definitely medieval in terms of its culture. I don't say that in a pejorative way. Despite the fact that there are cars and motorbikes and satellite phones, the vast majority of the population are uneducated and illiterate. It's a society very much based on tribe and kinship, and pretty small horizons. Also, it is an agrarian society: most of the population are farmers and the majority of those are tenant farmers. The landlords, in many cases, are absentee because of the fighting.

For centuries, Sangin has been a trading crossroads and it's still pretty significant in that respect. Sangin bazaar is our barometer of success: every time the number of shops in the bazaar increases, that's progress. I'm never good on numbers and statistics – although I'm constantly demanding them from my staff – but at the latest count, there were around about a thousand shops in the bazaar. It's definitely bustling at the moment.

You've got a huge variety of goods there, everything from some serious bits of technical hardware like large electricity transformers through to CDs and DVDs, and the little stalls play their wares at full volume. We try to encourage the patrols to spend a bit of money in there, which generates goodwill, but, to be frank, most goods are not particularly high quality. I haven't seen anything I'd be desperate to buy. They have this delicious long bread, about two feet long, which they cook in a wood oven, and huge amounts of vegetables, tomatoes, fruits, melons, all pretty seasonal. Not all the perfect shape and size that a British supermarket would demand. And always pomegranates. The area is littered with huge pomegranate orchards, these hawthorn-like trees with lots of low branches that are the bane of our lives in terms of providing cover for the enemy. The

Afghans are very proud of these pomegranates and I eat quite a lot with my Afghan counterparts, whether that be the district governor, or the Afghan Kandak commander.

Our biggest challenge here, bearing in mind that our operations are focused on the people not the enemy, is the whole business of Taliban intimidation. I need to have my troops located in places reasonably close to the people, so we can regularly patrol into a village or a group of compounds, engage with the population and be seen to be providing a persistent security presence: 'We're here to help, what do you need? Do you need wells, or a school? Can we refurbish your mosque?' Whatever it is. But if you disappear and don't come back for a week or two, the Taliban or their agents come in and the intimidation begins – for a start, they'll give people a hard time for talking to us. So I need my guys to engage with the people daily, to show we are here to stay.

FOB Jackson, where we're quartered, is nestled on the eastern bank of the Helmand river. We live in what we call HABs, hardened accommodation bunkers, which are huts made out of Hesco bastion. The facilities are pretty basic. We've got hundreds of us in there at the moment – and six showers, which produce water that's pumped out of the canal and filtered a bit.

We took over from the 2nd Battalion The Rifles. There was no major ceremony. We just did a handover, which was literally what we call a relief in place because obviously the work doesn't stop, and eventually, the locals noticed there was a different battle group in town.

Trouble started right away. The big thing about Sangin is the IEDs. Sangin has always had a high level of casualties. There isn't much by way of pitched battles. When you go out of your forward operating bases, the enemy will take it as an opportunity to kill you by laying IEDs around the place. They've identified, rightly, that on a straight force-on-force military fight, they're not going to match us and they'll probably get themselves done in. Unfortunately, all too regularly, somebody is blown up by an IED, and we have to protect ourselves against those, so the guys are out in body armour and helmets. I think the people accept this, although we'd much rather be dressed in berets, where we're much more approachable.

There are various types of IED. You have what is known as the victim-operated ones, which are dreadful things. Another type allows the Taliban to discriminate between civilians and military. They will dig a wire behind a compound wall or a bush, or wherever they can hide it. The wire can be a couple of hundred metres long or a few feet long, depending upon the terrain. When they see you coming past, they'll just connect the ends up to a battery.

The first casualty we had as a battle group was less than a couple of weeks after I took over. It was Staff Sergeant Olaf Schmid. You couldn't fail to know Schmid, he was one of those personalities who grabbed everyone's attention. He was bubbly and humorous, and just fully up for it. I remember the first time I met him was before I even started my handover. I happened to be waiting for a helicopter in Bastion – in fact, I'd gone to meet Rob Thomson, who I was going to be taking over from – and Staff Schmid and his team of EOD guys were transiting through as well. I remember Rob was full of praise: 'Nick, you've got to meet this guy, Staff Schmid, he's the greatest ATO alive.'

The info that there's been a casualty comes across from soldiers on the ground into our battle group operations room: 'Contact IED, wait out . . .' while they establish what casualties there have been and how serious they are.

Inevitably, amputations are one of the biggest threats to life with these IEDs, so that's the information you've got to get across first. That triggers a chain of events which goes all the way down to Camp Bastion, where there's a quick reaction helicopter. The minute they hear there's been an amputation, their objective is to get out to us as quickly as possible to lift the casualty off the ground.

In Staff Schmid's case, the whole place was showered in dust and debris after the explosion, so it wasn't quite clear for a while what had happened. Sadly, in his case, the communication was 'Man missing', which is one of the worst things because you don't know whether somehow insurgents have got hold of him or the body. There was a period of suspense when one was working out what was going on. But they found him and the message that came through was 'KIA', killed in action. That was our first death, and it was pretty devastating.

People are pretty subdued after something like that, but I'm afraid to say that almost right away its business as usual and we carry on.

Only a few days later, we lost Serjeant* Phillip Scott, and much as we all loved Staff Schmid, we had only been with him for a few weeks. Serjeant Scott was a long-serving member of the battalion and I think that probably hit people harder.

*The spelling of sergeant with a 'j' is unique to the Rifles.

Serjeant Scott was a lovely, charming guy, this huge, strong country boy from gamekeeper stock. I'm quite keen on a bit of shooting myself, so we always had good chats about country life, which was something I greatly enjoyed and will miss.

Rifleman Phil Allen from 2 Rifles was two days after Serjeant Scott and then Rifleman Sam Bassett from 4 Rifles was killed on 8 November. Then the next one was Rifleman Andrew Fentiman, who was on loan from the TA's 7 Rifles, out of Reading.

Either the day of a death or at sunset the following day we will all down tools and congregate on the helipad. The padre will lead a short service of remembrance and someone will read out a bit of a eulogy for the soldier or soldiers who have been killed. At the end the commanding officer will call out, 'Bugle Major, sound the advance,' and the bugle major, having done the 'Last Post' previously during the service, will sound the advance, and that's it, the service is finished, and we're off again.

We then had a month's gap, and it was the fifteenth of December that Lance Corporal David Kirkness and Rifleman James Brown were killed by a suicide bomber in Sangin, along with a couple of Afghans. I didn't know Rifleman Brown, but I'd met Lance Corporal Kirkness a few times. They were both in the same platoon as Serjeant Scott, which was the reconnaissance platoon.

Lance Corporal Michael Pritchard, from the Royal Military Police, was after Kirkness and Brown, and then shortly after that, Lance Corporal Christopher Roney was injured on 21 December, and died on the twenty-second, the same day that Lance Corporal Tommy Brown, who was attached from the

Paras, was blown up, and an interpreter was killed with him as well.

Then we had Rifleman Aidan Howell killed up in Kajaki on 28 December. He was a boisterous chap, full of high spirits and laughs, as most of them are. Despite being a relatively new arrival to the battalion, he was already operating with the C Company fire support group and he'd done very well with that. Sapper David Watson was killed on New Year's Eve. He was an engineer, part of the conventional munitions team, not necessarily known here as they rotate through, but I'd seen him around.

Corporal Lee Brownson and Rifleman Luke Farmer had been on a night patrol and come under contact from the enemy, but were moving back to the patrol base when they got caught in quite a big IED, and were blown up pretty comprehensively. We were hard hit by that. I manage people's careers from the time they are a corporal, so inevitably I'm going to know the corporals much better. I knew Corporal Brownson pretty well. He was a lovely chap, really going places. He was fairly mischievous, and he had a bit of history on him at times, but he was really capable. He was tactically very good, a good leader, and pretty shortly he would have been a platoon serjeant, which is the next level up.

Rifleman Peter Aldridge was A Company, 4 Rifles again. He was killed in an IED while on foot patrol. Then Lance Corporal Daniel Cooper was done for by an IED as well. Cooper I knew. I'd been down to the base after Brownson and Farmer had been killed and had a chat with him in the very sangar where Corporal Roney had been fatally wounded. But despite this,

Lance Corporal Cooper was chipper as you like. I was struck by how incredibly positive and energetic he'd been. I also related to him because he was from Hereford, where we have a house.

One learns a lot about leadership and motivation at times like these when terrible things are happening. A lot of the important things come back to standards of dress and discipline, which may seem ridiculously superficial and petty, especially as we're Rifles not Guardsmen. We don't need to have shiny boots or polished buttons – that's in fact why we have black buttons, so we don't have to polish them. And they're more tactical, not being shiny, which was the original reason. But take side-boards, for example. The Army regulation is that they must be no longer than halfway down the ear, but the guys like to mess around with their facial hair and express themselves through funny arrangements. As a commanding officer I don't want to be the bloke that's saying 'Sort yourself out, your sideboards are too long' or 'You look scruffy', but sometimes the platoon serjeant whose responsibility this really is will say, 'Oh well, the guys have had such a hard time, I'm just going easy on them.' But you don't trade the regulations for some sort of easing up of the challenges. The importance of self-discipline links into the grieving process as well. One's got to be tough to keep this show on the road; we can't all collapse into a heap of self-pity.

The last two were sadly killed a couple of days ago. Private Sean McDonald and Corporal John Moore were from B Company 1 Scots, when I was already back home, which was pretty miserable, although I didn't necessarily feel any different because I was here. What it meant for me was that I had to do at home what I always have to do, which is to put together a eulogy for them and write a letter of condolence to their families. The letter needs to reunite with their bodies at Lyneham this Friday.

I find these letters incredibly hard. For one thing, they take an awfully long time to write; clearly, one's got to be very thoughtful about what one says. I think my general objectives are to clarify for the family as much as possible what happened and try to put the context of what they were doing out in Sangin, which was working to prevent the oppression of the population out there and to provide opportunities for the place to get better. I appreciate some of this can be construed as an element of propaganda, but I think, particularly when you're writing eulogies and condolences, one's got to emphasise all the positive things they were doing. I try to talk about the events that led up to their deaths. One of the key things I like to be able to do is indicate that everything possible was done for them: the helicopter came in very quickly, the treatment was excellent, whether on the ground from his mates or if he made it back to the hospital in Bastion. I really try to address the issue as to whether he suffered or not, which is what families are probably going to want to know. I finish off by saying how much we appreciate his sacrifice, that we appreciate their sacrifice as a family, and that we are a regiment that remains on hand to support them. We're a family regiment.

Being back home on R & R introduces all the tensions between work and home life that one has to balance. I think my family would love me not to be in the Army for the two weeks I'm here. It's tough on the family. There's a lot of conflict about what I do on my R & R. As a previous CO once said to me, 'Life is very simple away on operations when one has a single focus.'

As a commanding officer there is always something going on, things which invariably involve people and their welfare. Two soldiers killed in action while I was away, two eulogies to write within twenty-four hours and two letters of condolence. I've got these two guys being repatriated to Lyneham on Friday. Corporal Cooper's being buried in Hereford the following Friday. I can't just hide away. But this is one of the things that comes with the responsibility. I'm the commanding officer of the battalion. It's a position where you are directly responsible for all the soldiers under your command. I'm extremely privileged and fortunate, both in career and personal terms to have it, and I don't see it as something I can switch off from.

However, we managed to escape for a long weekend to a lovely isolated cottage on a grouse moor up in Scotland, walking and looking at beautiful views, and playing games by the fire with the children and we managed to go *en famille* to an excellent production of *The Sound of Music* at the Edinburgh Playhouse.

But there was a bit of work to do on the letters and the eulogies, which did not exactly add to family harmony, and I also took time out to nip back into Edinburgh for a few hours to meet some very generous businessmen who are quarrying and crafting a large stone obelisk for our new memorial garden in the barracks. I also had a morning hosting General Sir Peter Wall, the Commander-in-Chief Land Forces, who had come to visit the battalion and its rear party, mainly in recognition of the large number of casualties we have received.

We lost two more men during my R & R: on Valentine's Day, 14 February, Rifleman Mark Marshall, who was from 6 Rifles down in Exeter and also a community support policeman, was killed instantly by an IED.

Following up on the incident, a patrol went back to that area and Sapper Guy Mellors from the engineer search team got caught by another IED. But that's part of the risk of all this, you can't leave places unvisited, and one just has to do it as safely and carefully as one can. Sadly, it didn't work out on that day.

In the end, time went all too quickly. Then it was packing the family in the car and driving the six hours down to Hereford, through the Birmingham snow, ready for Lance Corporal Cooper's funeral in Hereford Cathedral. It was hugely well attended and his family had asked me to do a reading, which I duly did. It was a poignant occasion and I did find it quite emotional, knowing Lance Corporal Cooper a bit more than I might most at his level, and being from Hereford myself. One is not entirely ready for the home-based ceremonial side of things while still in the middle of the tour, so it felt a little odd and, I have to say, that as I looked at the flag-draped coffin in the middle of the cathedral, I also felt the presence of our other dead lying there.

And that was it really; down to Brize Norton to fly back to Afghanistan. It had been a lovely break and I enjoyed the time with the family. But there was no sense of not wanting to go back, nor even a particular desire to stay a bit longer – just grateful for the time I had and a need to get back out there with the boys and finish the job.

The 3 Rifles Battle Group lost thirty men during their six-month tour of duty in Afghanistan, and I met up once again with Lieutenant Colonel Kitson back in England to hear about the rest of the men who had died in service.

On 25 February, Rifleman Martin Kinggett was on a patrol down on the northern 611, which is the main route that goes through Sangin, which we had essentially captured off the enemy to join up a number of our bases. The patrol came under contact from the enemy and Rifleman Borthwick was hit in the chest. As part of his treatment and evacuation, Rifleman Kinggett and others moved around to give covering fire and carry the attack back to the enemy, and while he was doing that, he got shot in the head.

Rifleman Carlo Apolis, originally from South Africa, was a great chap, a little bit older and wiser at twenty-eight years old, and very popular with the boys. While the Engineers were moving in to build and fortify a new compound, his team was occupying a roof to provide cover and he was hit in the chest by enemy small-arms fire while in a position overwatching a roof.

The next day, Corporal Richard Green was conducting vehicle checkpoints on Route 611, training and mentoring the Afghan Army. This inevitably meant being a bit more static, therefore presenting a bigger target. He was hit by accurate fire and died pretty instantly. He was a very capable soldier, ambitious, and had a lot going for him, and a lot he was probably going to achieve, so that was sad.

That was a difficult period for morale. Not only the tragedy of losing an up-and-coming NCO, but because Corporal Green had been shot on our doorstep by someone who was relatively professional – they'd got into a static fire position overlooking what we were doing and had taken an accurate shot. Previously one tended just to get cowboy shoots, where people would fire wildly at a patrol base.

A platoon very courageously went about conducting operations to try and flush out the guy who had shot Rifleman Green. There was a bit of a fear that a sharpshooter was on the loose. While the patrols were clearing the area from which Corporal Green had been shot, Rifleman Liam Maughan was in a position of overwatch on a roof, and that very tragically cost him his life. Rifleman Maughan was killed by a gunman, possibly the same sharpshooter. We had reports that this chap blew himself up laying an IED a few days later, which some might say was due justice.

Three days later, Rifleman Allott was killed. Allott was in a patrol base that was formerly the residence of a drug baron. It had the rather colourful name of Airport Lounge, as it had been garishly decorated and on the top a water tank had been built in the shape of an aeroplane.

Rifleman Allott was out at the front of the patrol with nothing but a metal detector to try and identify IEDs. These guys found the things in the first place and then brought in the EOD operators to dispose of them safely. But of course on all too many occasions the IEDs found our riflemen, and I'm afraid it was one of those.

After that we lost Lance Corporal Tom Keogh, who was in one of the new patrol bases we had built up along the road towards FOB Inkerman. These were a real thorn in the insurgents' side, because previously the Taliban had run illegal checkpoints on that road and they had been able to tax, intimidate and control anybody going in and out of the local bazaar. Putting in those patrol bases meant the Taliban were no longer able to do those checkpoints, so they were constantly firing at us, and on Sunday 7 March, unfortunately, a shot hit Corporal Keogh. If that wasn't bad enough, on the same day we lost Corporal Stephen Thompson, who was killed by an IED in the southern Green Zone.

So that was definitely a bad period, and you begin to start asking yourself a few questions when that goes on. The way I'd always seen it was that some of these casualties were kind of inevitable, an occupational hazard, because so many odds were not in our favour (although sometimes they were). We absolutely took the fight back to the enemy, and certainly caused plenty of casualties, but we wanted to make absolutely sure they were the right kind of casualties because the rules of engagement are all about the exercise of restraint, which was a key part of what we were doing. Inevitably that meant the enemy would sometimes get away with it, but galling as it was, it was preferable that an enemy got away because you weren't 100 per cent sure enough to engage him, rather than you killed someone who wasn't guilty, or caused any form of collateral damage.

We didn't have any more fatalities until 22 March when Serjeant Steven Campbell was killed by an IED down in the southern Green Zone. I don't like to favour one person over another, but to be honest this was a very difficult one for me. I was closely involved in managing his career and I liked him a lot. He was hugely forthright, married, with a ten-year-old son called Brandon, who was pretty much my son Thomas's age.

Rifleman Daniel Holkham was killed on 27 March. By that stage one was beginning to feel we were getting to the end of the tour, although there was absolutely no question of letting up or becoming more cautious or anything like that, which can happen. There'd been an IED in the wadi, and the bomb disposal team had been out and disposed of it, and Rifleman Holkham's patrol had been part of that. As the men patrolled back after the operation, a vehicle came driving up the wadi. Rifleman Holkham called to it to halt for a search. Rather than stopping, the vehicle sped up and veered towards him. In a split second it detonated – it was a suicide bomber and he blew himself up. Poor Rifleman Holkham was killed outright and a number of other guys were wounded, although thankfully not too seriously. Daniel Holkham had two brothers serving in the battalion. He had one brother in the recce platoon that was working with his company.

That was unfortunate, being so close to the end of the tour, but not as close as Rifleman Mark Turner who was our last fatality. That was up in Kajaki, on Sunday 4 April, Easter Day. Rifleman Turner was a Vallon man – that's the name of the metal detector we use – and he had built up quite a reputation as an IED hunter, and by the end of the tour he had racked up a pretty impressive number of IEDs. During a fighting patrol towards the enemy, he was clearing a new position for the soldiers to set down and he set off an IED and he was killed instantly. That was number thirty for our battle group, sadly.

And then it was time for us to go. Our transfer of authority date was 18 April, exactly six months after I took over from 2 Rifles. It was very much a relief in place. On 18 April we handed over control to the new guys from 40 Commando, Royal Marines; we took down our flag, they put up theirs, and off we disappeared.

MAJOR IAN LAWRENCE

'Out damned spot . . .'

I started being a Royal Welch Fusilier. The regiment is more than three hundred years old and had never been amalgamated until a few years ago when we were amalgamated with the Royal Regiment of Wales and now we're called the Royal Welsh. But we've retained our unique identity. Fifty per cent of my soldiers speak Welsh as their first language and half the battalion are called Jones, Williams or Jenkins, so we use the last two numbers of their regimental numbers in order to differentiate them, i.e. Williams 05 and Williams 22

Traditions are everything, aren't they? We have a regimental goat – not a mascot, you understand – who is part of the regiment. One of his ancestors charged the enemy at Bunker Hill in 1775, butted one of the Americans and was promoted in the field to lance corporal. We wear a flash of five overlapping black silk ribbons on the back of our tunic, which stems from the days when officers wore wigs and would grease their hair in a pigtail. The ribbons were sewn in to protect against any grease or white

229

powder falling on to the tunic. During the First World War, General Haig said, 'I want the Royal Welch to stop wearing their flash at the back, it's too conspicuous to German snipers.' But the King interceded and said, 'Don't worry, General, the enemy will never see the backs of the Royal Welch Fusiliers.'

The reason why I joined the Army was to command on a battlefield, that was the challenge and impetus for me. You've got people being injured or killed, bullets are flying, bombs are dropping, there's complete chaos – and trying to lead your way out of that situation has got to be the biggest challenge on the planet. I wanted to find out whether I could do it.

Being in a platoon or a company where you have been involved in fighting transcends all other things. It is the highest honour and privilege that man can become involved in. Operations are amazing, unbelievable experiences. There's nothing like them for gelling soldiers, senior NCOs, the officers together – we're a team then, a very close-knit team.

The best tour I did was in Gorazde in Bosnia. Physically, it was a terrible posting, but I look back on it with fondness.

We were not there representing the Royal Welsh Fusilier cap badge – had we been, there might have been a different story. On this tour we were wearing the blue helmets of the United Nations. As a blue helmet, you can fight to protect yourself and other people, but you can't take the fight to the enemy. Also, everything's got to be transparent. For instance, we couldn't take code sheets with us to speak in code on the radio, although when things got very difficult we got around that by speaking Welsh. We were there supposedly to uphold the peace. We had observation posts around the enclave and the idea was to stop the Serbians from coming in with any weaponry.

The summer of 1995 was a time when the Balkans were in turmoil. Srebrenica, then Zepa, had fallen to the Serbs, and tens of thousands of Muslims were being rounded up and massacred. Gorazde was the last Muslim enclave, although it was completely surrounded by the Serbs, who were hell-bent on coming into the enclave and killing as many Muslims as they could.

Gorazde was in bad shape. Most of the buildings had been burned down during the ethnic cleansing and the few left were pockmarked with shells and bullets. Virtually no glass remained in any of the windows, there was no electricity in the town, no industry and the school frequently had to close because Serbian snipers were shooting Muslim kids as they walked to school. Because virtually all the men had been killed, the town consisted mostly of women and children, who were terrified for their lives. The majority were very ill. They were living on meagre rations and looked malnourished, with sallow, sunken cheeks. To be honest, it felt like a Holocaust scenario, that you were on the edge of Auschwitz.

I was there six months. The first three months were OK. The last two to three months were pretty bad. We were taking a hammering most days from Serbian artillery, so we dug trenches and lived underground and in armoured Saxon vehicles. We got the engineer to make a big scoop in the ground and we put in an ISO container and then earth on top of that, which was the best protection we could give. Most of the ops rooms had to be in Portakabins because no communications could work below ground. The Serbians prevented rations from coming in, so we went down to half rations. For weeks we were having just two meals a day of dried pasta. Things were really tough.

But a curious thing starts to happen when things get bad – a black sense of humour develops, started by the boys who've got an absolutely wicked sense of humour. When the chips are really down, they'll start to come up with cracking jokes. Once you've laughed together, facing horror, you're on a different level. You're a brotherhood, and we would fight and die for each other. There was no question about it.

You know each of your soldiers intimately. You know how he does his administration, you know how he polishes his boots, how he eats his food – even what he eats first on his plate. Once you've lived very close to him, you can smell him, you can taste him, you know what he's thinking. A bond starts to develop and doesn't get broken, even as the years roll by. If I had people who were in Gorazde with me in this room now, I would immediately snap back to our relationship as it was then. We'd look at each other and we'd understand one another, and it would be like nothing else.

Something like thirty of our soldiers were captured by the Serbs as prisoners of war on that tour. I remember the first time it happened with ten of our men. One of the corporals under my command called me on the radio and said, 'Sir, this is the situation. We've had some firefights, but we're now at our last. I'm surrounded by Serbs, outnumbered at roughly ten to one, with small arms, and a heavy machine gun pointed at us. They're fifty metres away from the OP now, sir. Do you want me to try and fight my way out of this situation?'

On operations your training clicks in. For example, when I'm in a difficult scenario where fighting is going on, I will take a chill pill, slow my voice down and think methodically because it's really important you're seen to be absolutely unflappable.

I remember saying to him, 'Corporal Parry, you've done the best you can. I want no man killed. You are to put down your weapons and surrender.' He said to me, 'Sir, thank you for saying that. See you when we meet back in the UK. Sir, we're about to be captured.'

Had I not ordered him to surrender, I know he would have fought, and he would have killed a lot of Serbs. But they would have killed a lot of our guys and if you're fighting a fight, you want to fight it on the terms that suit you, on the grounds of your own choosing, with the tactics and the weaponry of your choosing. I still say I made the right call. Of those ten men who were captured, they all made it back to the UK, they're all still alive and they've all now got family.

There was one key thing that I picked up from a padre who had been out in the Falklands. 'You will see atrocities,' he said – and I did – 'but the thing to do when you see blood and gore and guts exposed in a battle situation is to put those horrible feelings in a box at the back of your mind and close the lid. You can deal with all of the horror later.' And that works for me.

Injuries can be bizarre or surreal. For example, there'll be pieces of limbs that you recognise lying on the ground – you know, a finger or a thumb. Oh my God, there's a hand there. The look of death on a man's face on the battlefield, where he obviously died in a state of pain, is not a pleasant sight. People know when they are reaching their last few moments and will get anxious as their body starts to close down. You see the look

233

afterwards: of horror and anxiety. There's no drifting away with a smile on their face.

There are terrible noises. There's lots of sighing. If they've been injured in their lungs and the blood is frothing up, there can be gurgling, which can be quite noisy in itself. They can be screaming. They're uncomfortable. They're writhing. Sometimes, when a young soldier has been shot, he's simply crying for his mother every few seconds until he just drifts away.

We value life in our country, but you go to parts of the world where life means nothing. For instance, I met some Chetnik Serbs as we were patrolling around the observation posts, who invited a group of us into their house for some bread and coffee. We were talking about us being fellow soldiers together and that sort of thing. Then the conversation changed to them saying they were looking forward to coming into the town to murder as many Muslims as they could, and raping the women, 'because they breed like rats'. At that stage you realise the depth of evil you're dealing with. I put my coffee down, my soldiers did the same, and I looked at their leader and said, 'You're not a soldier, you are an animal. I despise you.' I think those Serbs knew I was right, but they had by now gone too far down the path of murder and destruction to turn back. They were lost souls on the edge of the battlefield.

Eventually, humanity will catch up with those Chetniks. They will end up in a gutter somewhere or they will be dealt with by some criminal court. People who chose to ignore humanity, no matter on which side, well, it will come to haunt them. I've seen very macho chaps kill people on operational tours and almost all of them have to deal with the aftermath. They cry like babies, particularly when they come home. It takes an awful long time to come to terms with what they have done.

Just this past weekend I was at home and my twelve-year-old daughter was learning the Lady Macbeth speech, the one where she's washing her hands constantly: 'Out damned spot.' I was struck by that. All those centuries ago, Shakespeare realised that humanity catches up with people who have been involved in some form of illicit killing and they will be punished.

We got to know the Muslims very well, particularly some of the children. A boy called Addis, and his sister Adisa, used to come up to me when I was patrolling around and tug at my trousers or pull my shirt in a jokey way. They'd invite me to come to their farm. They had no father, no uncles or brothers, no males in their family were left at all – everyone was dead, and whenever I got anything, sweets or batteries, and that sort of thing, I'd give them to those two.

But as the tour was developing, I recognised I was becoming too close to these children. I knew the way the boy was looking at me that I was becoming a surrogate father to him, and I had to break away because if I am biased towards any one family, then I am not being impartial. And I was there as a soldier, not a child minder. One day I said, 'Look, sorry Addis, I've got a job to do.' He looked as if he'd done something terribly wrong.

One morning I'm driving down the road in a Land Rover and there's the young girl, Adisa, walking to school with her brother beside her on a rickety old bicycle. Someone starts shooting at them. The girl and boy both scream and the boy falls off his bicycle. I manoeuvre the Land Rover into a position where they can take shelter behind it. The children are hysterical and I drive

235

off with them to the school, which is just an empty fabric of a building, with no teaching materials or anything, and I put them into the care of the headmaster.

About a week later, we dug in at night, with heavy .50 cal machine guns and sniper rifles in a series of positions, cammed up so they couldn't be seen. We asked the headmaster to open the school one more time. Reluctantly, he did so. As the sun came up in the morning, mist was still lying in the valley bottom. Children started walking to school, and as they did, they started being shot at again from the valley bottom. We absolutely malleted the Serbian positions, really nailed them, with massive weight of fire, sniper rifles going in, machine-gun fire chopping up their bricks as they were trying to hide. It's still ringing in my ears. We killed in the order of ten Serbians. A few hours later when the mists rose, we could see the Serbians loading up the dead bodies on to mules and taking them away. The school stayed open from that moment onwards and whenever anyone shot at any of the schoolchildren, we absolutely hammered them, so that a very clear message was sent out.

In the end we successfully protected the enclave. We would have fought tooth and nail to save the Muslims, there's no question of that. Gorazde was not going to go the same way as Srebrenica and Zepa. The Serbs got fairly close, though. But it ended phenomenally. After various diplomatic talks, the Dayton Accord was signed and the Muslims were saved.

Never ask a soldier if he's killed anyone. My children have asked me and I've told them that's the one question you never ever ask a soldier because he would then be relating a story to a civilian who doesn't understand the context in which that event occurred. It would be unfair on that civilian as much as it would be unfair on the soldier.

When you come back from an operational tour, you have a period of time called decompression, during which you try to calm down and ease back into normal life again. The pressure cooker that you were in in operations is alleviated by trivial things, like taking the dog out for a walk or watching television. We've all got wives who are very good at managing us. My wife knows: 'Right, Ian's going to be a bit unsettled when he first comes home,' so she will fend off all family and friends for four or five days, and just allow me to get to know where everything is in the house and relate to the family again.

But, being honest, everything seems completely irrelevant when you come back – not important, irritating really. Conversations are going on and you're thinking, I'm listening to you, but do you know what? It doesn't matter what sort of car you are interested in buying or which restaurant you might go to this evening, I just don't care – you don't understand what really matters and what's just trivia.

Once you've been in an intense life-and-death situation, it always stays with you. I can still remember absolutely everything I saw in Gorazde. I can play it back, like a film reel, whenever I like.

Here's a freeze-frame moment: I'm patrolling through an area of Gorazde. A man of about seventy is tending some vegetables out of a dried, rubbish piece of ground because he's probably starving. A sniper shot rings out and this old man collapses on the ground in front of us, shot in the heart. He dies within a few seconds. He happened to have a cigarette in the corner of his mouth and somehow it stays there. He was an elderly man, trying to grow something to eat. What does it mean? Nothing.

MAJOR WILLIAM LEWIS*

'It comes with cruise control . . .'

As a nine-year old, I watched the film *Wild Geese*, with Richard Burton and Roger Moore – my mum went berserk about it when she found out – and from then on I was fixated with soldiers jumping out of aeroplanes.

We had an Army cadet force at school. I went to see the school liaison officer when I was only thirteen or fourteen and he pulled out a brochure with a helicopter on the cover. I said, 'Oh, I didn't realise the Army had helicopters.'

'Yes, that's the Army Air Corps,' he said. 'Do you want to visit?'

Of course, I said yes, and I was invited to sit in the back of a Scout helicopter.

The Scout had a sort of bubble window, so you could properly see out and I remember looking out of the window while this thing lifted up into the air, and seeing all the grass being blown around while we were floating. The pilot went to fly away, the nose tipped forward, and I thought, Oh my gosh, we are going to hit the ground. Then, all of a sudden, it was as if the hand of God lifted us into the sky. Fantastic. Big smile on my face. And that was it, I was hooked.

The first vehicle you are given when you are learning to fly is a fixed-wing Firefly, a little yellow two-seater aeroplane in which you learn physically how to drive the thing around the sky. You find out what the controls do: up, down, left, right, pedals, power, and so on. Then you build that into flying a circuit and you fly round in what we call a square, and land. Can you navigate? Can you get from A to B, while doing all the other things you need to do when you fly? This is where flying becomes like that game children play: can you pat your head, rub your tummy and say the alphabet backwards? Can you fly and also map-read, talk on the radio, monitor all your instruments, look out the window to make sure you're not going to fly into anything, and have enough what we call 'capacity to be able to deal with the unexpected', like all of a sudden the engine bursting into flames?

You'll need to learn how to hover. You find a big field somewhere and the instructor sets you up in hover. He will then say, 'Right, I am now giving you the pedals,' and you must keep the aircraft pointing straight, which is what the pedals do. OK, fine. Then he gives you another control, the cyclic, which in essence controls the direction you want to go. Finally, you get given the collective, which is a lever that literally puts more pitch on to the blades, so you can go up and down. The three of them together equalise each other and enable you to hover, or 'transition to the hover' as it's called.

It is actually quite easy to hover: if you watch somebody hovering, they hardly move the controls. It all seems effortless. But trainees tend to establish the hover and then a second or two later, a sort of negative feedback loop develops, they start creating more and more of an error, until the instructor has to take the controls, settle them down and get them back again. In the end you will master it, it's just like riding a bike. How do you teach somebody to ride a bike? Well, you don't, the novice has to pedal and eventually he will balance. Hovering is exactly the same.

At this point you are basically a civilian pilot, and the intention next is to turn you into a military pilot, using a Squirrel helicopter. The pilots' course is much more the tactical application of what you have learned, so dealing with formation flights, talking to air operation controlling artillery fires. You're layering in an electronic warfare threat, with other aircraft moving around you, and fast air (jets) above. You also need to get from A to B, and be at B plus or minus seven seconds to the set time, which is what you would ultimately be doing as a trained pilot in an operational aircraft.

You then convert from Squirrel to Lynx, and that's when the fun starts. Fundamentally, they're the same vehicle, in that they're both helicopters – but in the same way that a Ferrari and a Mini are both cars. The Squirrel is like a Ford Escort – it does everything that you want it to, but it is bland beyond belief. The Lynx is like a very fast car, maybe like a smart Alfa Romeo, or something that isn't that reliable mechanically, where the electrics break on it from time to time, but it's bloody quick and it looks beautiful. The Lynx is a fantastic aircraft. It is the fastest helicopter in the world. It has been over two hundred miles an hour, which for a helicopter is pretty amazing. It is also incredibly manoeuvrable. It has two engines and a whole raft of new dials and switches in the ceiling. It takes another two months of training to convert on to a Lynx helicopter.

The difference between Lynx and Apache is also incredible. In a Lynx helicopter you are sat side by side, like you do in a car, whereas in an Apache you are sat one in front of another, like in a toboggan. Or imagine the front- and back-seaters in the movie *Top Gun*. You can fly the Apache from both cockpits. You can fire all the weapon systems and operate all the radar from both cockpits, but the front-seat is more often than not the mission commander because he has got better access to the sight and sensors, and the back-seat is the driver. From a crewing perspective, you would think the two of you not being able to see each other, plus only hearing each other on a monotone intercom, would be a huge disadvantage, but when you start your course, a psychologist comes in and tells you that communication is 70 per cent body language, 20 per cent tone of voice and only 10 per cent the spoken word.

It's very hard not to sound naff when describing an Apache, but it's absolutely awesome to fly. First of all, there are the little things, like it comes with cruise control and there is a nice little lumbar back support too. Also, it's got air conditioning, which makes a massive difference. I mean, without sounding too precious, imagine flying on operations in Afghanistan, running out to your aircraft with a helmet and body armour, and flying low-level very fast: sweat is dripping into your eyes, which are stinging, and you are constantly trying to wipe the sweat away. It is a distraction, whereas air conditioning means you can focus purely on the task at hand.

The best thing of all about the Apache is the weapon systems. It is a gunship. You have got a 30mm gun, which fires ten rounds a second, and in Afghanistan it is without doubt the weapon of choice because it can deliver a high rate of fire and is very accurate to the target. I can slave the gun to wherever my head is looking, so I can look, pull the trigger, and the rounds will fire where I am looking. That's because the Apache has got a head-up display that bolts to your helmet, and it moves with your head and has got all of your flying information: how fast you are flying, navigation information, weapon information and so on, right in your eye, the point being that you can take all this information with you and use the helmet as a sight system in its own right.

You have also got rockets and missiles. You can carry rocket pods of nineteen rockets per pod. There are various different warheads you can put on the rocket, from a point-detonating high explosive to a flechette, which is a little tungsten dart. We also have the hellfire missile that can fire out to eight kilometres. It has two types of warhead: a point-detonating charge designed to destroy tanks and an enhanced blast warhead, which will collapse a building. You can have it laser guided and the missile will just follow to the end of the laser spot. It is a true fire-and-forget missile in that once it leaves the rails, it will go to wherever you have programmed it to go.

With all those buttons, it's incredibly easy for people who are quick with their fingers to use the weapon systems. The twenty-five-year-old sergeant or lieutenant from the PlayStation generation will find it's just like playing a computer game. And that's why fast jets and helicopters have gone down that route. So pulling the trigger on somebody is exceptionally easy – although you use your left trigger finger rather than your right trigger finger, which can take a long while to learn.

In Afghanistan the squadron is split down into a rostered system, so there's an IRT crew, an immediate response team and when somebody phones 999 to say, 'We are in contact here, help,' we will scramble to get in an aircraft. The back-seat runs to the aircraft and gets it started, while the commander will dive into the ops tent, get a brief and then launch. We can be airborne in minutes from the initial call.

Information is key. The most important thing is confirming where the friendly forces are located and where the enemy forces are. Initially, as we are flying, we'll speak to what we call a JTAC, joint tactical air control, who is a guy on the ground with a radio checking in with him and trying to build up our situational awareness of what is going on on the ground.

Take one mission we flew recently. We were flying up to Musa Qala, which isn't far from Camp Bastion. We checked in on the ground with the JTAC, who was literally on the company commander's shoulder, and had the situation update. Basically, there was a patrol of Paras who had taken one casualty – he had been shot in the arm, but was fine and didn't need a helicopter to take him out. But they had another section that had been pinned down, and they had called back through their own radios for air aviation support. We checked in with them: 'I am an Apache, *this* is the weapons we are carrying and *this* is the playtime we can give you,' playtime being how long I have got. We had two hours forty-five minutes, so we were fine, but it's important that the guys on the ground know at what point we are going to disappear.

I spoke to the commander, who was being pinned down. Sometimes the soldiers themselves don't know where they are –

they could be in the bottom of a trench somewhere. The guy I spoke to was saying to me, 'We are being engaged approximately two hundred metres to the north-west. We have got accurate small-arms fire pinning us down,' which made my life easy because straight away I can put that grid into the aircraft and slave all my optics. So I am now looking at his position through the TADS (target acquisition designated sight). This is when I can use the aircraft sensors to pick up hotspots and I can see bodies. At that point, my back-seat says to me, 'Yes, I can see movement in that bush line,' and we discuss what we can see.

There is then a sort of pregnant pause in the aircraft, where we are thinking, Right, rules of engagement. All crews are permanently concerned about the rules of engagement, which say when you can fire and when you can't. Basically, it's about the right of self-defence, so if I see somebody firing at my guys on the ground, I can engage them. I told the guy on the ground what I was going to do and I then engaged the enemy with the 30mm gun. We let the dust settle, literally, and waited for the JTAC to give what they call 'battle damage assessment'. They'll say, 'Stand by for BDA,' while I wonder, 'Will they want us to re-engage?'

Pulling the trigger in an Apache is hardly fixing bayonets. You are not seeing the direct consequences of an attack like an infantry soldier would see it, but being able to engage somebody with either a missile or the gun doesn't bother me because it really allows us to support the boys on the ground properly. I feel quite proud I am able to do something to stop further casualties to those boys, so they can live to fight another day. Army helicopters are flown by soldiers for soldiers, so I am very happy to be directed by the guys on the ground as to what they want me to do. I remember being back in the camp later that day meeting the 3 PARA soldiers we had helped out, who said, 'Fucking hell, was that you today? That was awesome, thank you.'

One of our duties is to protect the Chinook helicopters, so now you have an Apache flying in a circle above the top of them to escort them in, and if you see a puff of smoke, the Apache would then suppress that position quickly. A Chinook is predominantly there to do heavy-duty lifts on a battlefield, moving ammunition or troops.

The Apache pilots have great respect for the Chinook pilots because, to be frank, they are putting themselves in harm's way. There is this kind of mutual respect between Chinook pilots, who are RAF, and Apache pilots. A Chinook has got very little protection in terms of firepower. It is very slow landing or taking off and so prone to being mortared, quite often taking bullets – while we have all the bombs and bullets, and are sat outside of the threat band as we call it.

There is no real physical pressure flying the Apache, but there's mental pressure. Having to react very quickly to what's going on over quite a long period of time, your concentration levels are sustained at high levels and, coupled with the responsibility of what you are doing, you get incredibly tired, and it's not uncommon for guys who have been strapped in for eight hours to fall asleep almost as soon as they climb out of the aircraft. They just shut down mentally.

It was wonderful to be back at the end of the last tour. My daughter was asleep when I got home and I toyed with the idea of waking her up as I wanted to give her a hug, but after six months away, I thought she would probably go, 'Who the hell are you?' and start screaming, and it would all be too much. So I spent about an hour sitting on a chair next to her cot, just looking at her, thinking how she had changed and how beautiful she was.

LIEUTENANT COLONEL CHARLIE MACFARLANE

'The abuse we suffered was awful . . .'

Well, I joined at the age of fifteen, straight from school in Scotland, a place called Falkirk, just outside Stirling. My father had been in the Argyll and Sutherland Highlanders (Argylls) during the war, so that seemed to be the logical choice of regiment for me. I was pretty young and naive at the time. I didn't think too much about what I was doing, but I didn't fancy hanging around where I lived and thought the Army would show me the world.

My first sight of 'the world' was Northern Ireland. At that time, in the 1970s, it was quite a scary place to be. But I really wanted to go there because what you don't want as a soldier is to be someone who hasn't been on operations – it's like training to be an athlete and never running a race.

So we went over to Northern Ireland and were billeted in North Howard Street, between the Falls Road and the Shankill Road, in some godforsaken old Victorian mill that had been turned into a base. Our job was basically to keep the peace between the Catholics and the Protestants, who were setting out to kill each other. There were no policemen, anarchy was on the streets, and there were some very misguided and nasty people.

We didn't have to wait long for action. My first actual contact was on our first patrol. We had just left the base and moved on to the Falls Road, when suddenly we received Armalite and Thompson sub-machine-gun fire. After initial confusion we moved very quickly to try and cut off the gunmen's escape route – often they used to go to ground in people's houses, so we searched all around the neighborhood. But to be honest, in this case we weren't successful. They got clean away.

We were fired at a number of times during that tour. There were quite a lot of what you would call 'cowboy gunmen', guys who just pointed a weapon around the corner and fired a scattering of ammunition at you. Unlike today's Taliban, and the Iraqi militia, the IRA didn't stand and fight, the IRA tended to shoot and run very fast.

One day we got a tip there was a car loaded with a thousand pounds of explosive in the boot. We'd been told the registration, so we were looking for that car, and as we came round a corner, there it was, just sitting there. It was an old Zephyr, with its four flashers on – why they did that, I'll never know.

We had to evacuate the civilian population, then clear the roads and cordon off the area, and block the end of Falls Road – all the time wondering, How long before this thing goes off? The timers they used were hardly state-of-the-art digital. We had to get everyone out of the line of sight of the bomb because if the bomb can see you, then it can kill you.

That was quite an experience for a youngster of eighteen

because suddenly you're responsible for other human beings. The ATO, the ammunition technical officer, who defuses bombs, arrived, but before he could even get suited up, the thing went off. It didn't kill anyone, thankfully, but it shook the whole street. We were a good bit away from it, but we felt the shock: it reverberated through your bones, through your organs, and entered every cavity in your body. God knows what it must be like to be closer to it. I guess it would tear you to pieces.

As a young soldier, I thought it was all exciting, but as an older man now, looking back, I realise it was bloody dangerous.

Years later, in the 1990s, I went to Palace Barracks in Holywood, Belfast, as the quartermaster. The battalion spent two years there as resident, which meant we stayed with our families. Over two marching seasons the battalion was involved in some of the most lethal public disorder since the early 1970s and was heavily involved in the Holy Cross School stand-off, where our soldiers had to escort Catholic children to school every morning through a torrent of hate. I have to say, it was a very distasteful experience for most of the soldiers involved.

Over six years' operational experience in Northern Ireland I have seen some terrible things, but I think one of the worst things I experienced was a really nasty situation just off the Falls Road, where we had tried to arrest someone and they weren't for being arrested. The women poured out into the street and I'll never forget the hatred in the eyes of those women. They were old enough to be my mother, but the abuse we suffered was awful. We were spat on, had urine thrown over us, really awful things.

I have seen dead bodies. I've seen the aftermath of the terrible sectarian murders that took place over the 1970s. In the Shankill Road area, a gang called the 'Shankill Butchers' instigated a reign of terror against the Catholics and anyone unlucky enough to fall into their hands. We found a body thought at the time to be one of their victims. His head had been bashed against the corner of a skip before his throat had been cut. I've seen guys with their kneecaps drilled off with portable drills. Those things didn't really affect me. We just got on with it. I've seen the aftermath of bombs – once you've seen a dead body after a bomb blast, I don't think any dead body you see thereafter is really going to affect you. But the hatred of these women, well, I'd never felt that hatred before. It shocked me because it was coming from mothers. Even today it still shocks me whenever I think back on it.

I'm now fifty-three. After nearly forty years' service, I'll be leaving the Army next year. I think it will be difficult in so much as it is a complete step change in my life and I'm trying to prepare for it as best I can. All my career, from boy soldier to Lieutenant Colonel, which is a fair few hurdles to jump, there's always been a mission, a goal, that I've set myself, and now my goal must be to resettle and move to civilian street. Every two years I have moved house, moved location, but I long for stability, so does my wife. She's looking forward to moving into our house up in Scotland, although I think she's dreading me being around all the time.

But I'm looking forward to it. Forty years is a long time to do anything and I'm reaching the end of my usefulness as a frontline soldier. Last year I was in Afghanistan with ISAF, the International Security Assistance Force. That was tiring, and I realised I'd begun to reach my physical limitations as a soldier.

I think there's a time when you should say, 'I've had a good run, enough is enough,' and leave on a high.

It's been a fantastic career for me. I've been fortunate to have been commissioned, to go on and be promoted, and as a late-entry officer, coming from the ranks, lieutenant colonel is the highest I can reach. So yeah, I've had a fantastic career and loved every minute.

A few years ago, I had to change my Argyll cap badge, which was very hurtful because that cap badge is linked to hundreds of years of history. My father wore the same cap badge, as did my uncle, who died as a Japanese POW on the Burma to Siam railway and whose remains lie in the Kanchanaburi war cemetery in Thailand – which is a huge, emotional thing. But I got over it, because I'm an old soldier, and I do what I'm told, basically. It was less stressful for some of the younger soldiers, who didn't have relatives in the regiment before and did not really know much about the Argylls, and what effect losing that cap badge meant, but they will in time.

SERGEANT CHRIS RICHARDS

'A nice letter off Prince Charles . . .'

Don't get me wrong, I love the Army, I loved everything about it, but I was spending such a lot of time away from the family, and I thought, I want to see my children grow up, so I got out.

But then the thing was, if I wasn't out working, the wife would be, and sometimes we'd both be working, so the kids were being taken from pillar to post, and we realised we had spent more quality time together as a family while I was in the Army. The final straw was when one of my kids had a toothache and I was trying to get him into a dental practice, and it was: 'We're full in this area, you've got to drive twenty miles to another one.' When I was in the Army, we used an army dentist, and it was done immediately.

So I decided to come back, and because I was out for just under a year, and had left the regiment on good terms, I was welcomed back with open arms.

The first time I went out on a patrol in Iraq, I saw the way some of the people lived, and it opened my eyes.

We were just a kilometre or two outside of Basra, driving through what was basically a rubbish dump, and seeing children living among all this rubbish, broken bottles and faeces on the ground, with no shoes on their feet. It's a sad state when children have to do that and I felt so sorry for them. But it got me thinking, and when I came back to the UK for my R & R, the wife and I hatched an idea. When I flew back out to Iraq, I brought a suitcase filled with my children's old shoes, loads of pairs, welly boots and everything. They might not all fit, but I thought, Doing something is better than doing nothing. On my next patrol, I stopped outside this settlement, called over one of the ladies and gave her all these shoes and her eyes lit up.

Telic 11 was very quiet at first. We were doing various patrols in the Challenger 2s and then an Iraqi operation came in called Charge of the Knights: we were told there was someone of interest in a certain part of Basra. We were going to go after key militiamen there and take all the weapons that could be found.

This particular day, my troop leader was on R & R, and my troop corporal then usually led. That's Marco, who's a really good lad. I said to him, 'Marco, I'll lead tonight if you want,' just to give him a break from leading for once and he said, 'Yes, fine.' So that night there was myself as the lead tank, then a Scots Guards Warrior behind me, with some Iraqi and American Special Forces in the rear. The rest of the tanks were behind us to give a ring of steel around the area of interest.

As we were going in, we got a call over the radio saying there might possibly be sniper fire, so I closed down my hatch. Then I was told there might be a roadblock in place and to use whatever means possible to get through, and if that meant using my

120mm main armaments, then so be it. I pulled short of an area that was blocked off and, looking around it in the sights, I made sure there were no hotspots or anything suspicious. I realised I could get around it, so there was no need to use the 120mm. I pushed on with the operation, got to a roadblock and then there was this massive explosion. I stopped the tank, and my priority then was the safety of the crew. I made sure that my driver, gunner and operator were all fine, and it was then a case of talking to them over the intercom to make sure each function of the tank was OK:

'Gunner, have you still got all the controls of the gun?'

'Driver, can we still move backwards and forwards?'

'Operator, what's happening?'

Then I checked the vehicle – no problems – although obviously we couldn't see if there was any damage to the outside.

Something like that gives you a little bit of a shake, but we carried on and a few seconds later a second device went off. I went through the procedure again and everything was fine. Came across a couple of hotspots, and engaged with 7.62s and a chain gun to disrupt them. Continued pushing on. There was another roadblock about a hundred metres in front and I got told again over the radio: 'Use your one-twenty.' But I decided not to because I thought if I use my main armament, I would probably end up causing huge collateral damage. I used the 7.62mm again and pushed through the roadblock. Then the third and biggest explosion went off just in front of the tank and blew my commander's hatch open, although that was probably my fault because I obviously hadn't secured it tightly enough in the first place. There was all this dust in my eyes and I couldn't see anything for what felt like a lifetime, but was probably only a few seconds. For the third time I made sure everyone was OK. The vehicle was fine and as I pushed past the third IED, two further ones went off just to my rear, which I suppose were aimed at my vehicle. The Warrior behind took a little bit of damage. Finally reached my objective, which was a crossroads about two hundred metres away from the house of interest. Held the position, the relevant agencies went in and did what they had to do, and I then turned the tank around and pushed back into camp.

It turns out that everyone had been listening in on the radio, so they knew what had happened to us, and told us we were awesome. But I just did my job. I was in a massive seventy-ton tank, which will take quite a bit of pounding before it breaks, and so I thought nothing of it. A lot of people came over that night to have a look at the tank. It was good to get the younger lads to see the impacts we took and that the armour did its job and saved any penetration to the tank. Actually, I thought, Bloody hell, I'm glad I was in a Challenger because if it was anything else, it probably would have been pretty much destroyed. The Challenger is an awesome bit of kit. It's probably the best tank in the world with everything it's got on it, all the fighting systems, the armaments, the armour – and it packs a mighty punch. It probably saved my life and the crew's life.

I'm now based at ATR Bassingbourn, down in Cambridgeshire, which is a training regiment for new recruits coming into the British Army. A few months ago, the commanding officer called me into his office, along with a young infantry officer. We marched in and all the officers commanding, the majors and senior officers from ATR Bassingbourn were there, which was a bit of a surprise. The CO said, 'Right, stand at ease,' and he then stood up and read out this infantry officer's citation for what he did in Afghanistan.

It was amazing what this bloke did. He was in a firefight and gave the order to fix bayonets, and then he pretty much had one-on-one combat with the enemy. He didn't get any major decorations, but he got a mention in dispatches, which I guess is an award in itself. Then the CO read out my citation and I thought, Well, what I did was nothing compared to this guy, but, crikey, I might get a mention in dispatches too, but it came out that I'd been awarded the Military Cross. Everyone in the office clapped, but I was gobsmacked, speechless. I just didn't know what to say. Fortunately, there were a couple of bottles of port on the table and we all had a few glasses.

Well, it's a major honour really and a real suprise. I think I got the award for taking the decision not to use my main armament and destroy civilians or flatten the area around there.

Anyway, since then I've had letters from all sorts of people, including a nice letter off Prince Charles, who's Colonel-in-Chief of the regiment, just saying how proud he was that someone from his regiment was awarded the Military Cross. I've put all the letters in a box, kept away nice and safe for my children to look at when they get a bit older.

I had to go to Buckingham Palace to get my award. I took the wife and my two children and we made a few days of it in London. We saw a show, *Grease*, which I probably enjoyed more than the children, and went out for a meal. I got my award from Prince Charles.

Being at ATR Bassingbourn, I miss the lads and the closeness of the regiment – the Royal Dragoon Guards are like family. Ask anyone, we're all incredibly close. Also, I'm pretty well gutted that I'm missing the next operational tour into Afghanistan. But I feel I'm doing my part training the new lads coming into the British Army as they have to start somewhere.

Official citation accompanying Military Cross for Sergeant Chris Richards, Royal Dragoon Guards

In spite of significant threats Sergeant Richards commanded a lead tank with outstanding nerve, determination and exemplary gallantry in the face of the enemy.

Without his resolve to continue the advance, in spite of five IED attacks of which three were direct strikes, the operation would have ground to a halt before it started.

BRIGADIER JAMES STEVENSON
'First prize in the lottery of life . . .'

I had just finished a particular job in Northern Ireland, so I'd missed going out to Iraq with my battalion and was joining them literally in the desert in Saudi Arabia, for what was known as Operation GRANBY – the First Gulf War. Officially, I was going out as a battle casualty replacement as my predecessor had been shot in an accident in training. We've since had the Second Gulf War, we've had Afghanistan – it's now no longer strange to say you're off to the desert. But then a heavy-armoured offensive operation in the desert was a massive shock to the system, and a real excitement.

We landed in Al Jubail on the east coast of Saudi Arabia, and when I got off the plane, the first sensation was the smell of heat, which took me back twenty-one years to when we used to live in Bahrain: my father was in the Royal Navy and we were posted out there. If I closed my eyes, I could have been getting off the plane again, aged eight, back from school in the UK.

I got to the processing station at the other end, which was in this enormous hangar, and was waiting in a long queue to be put on to the database to say I had arrived in theatre, when I saw a good old friend of mine, Bill Sutherland, who was our man in Al Jubail processing people through. He marched down the line until he saw me, and very officially and loudly said, 'Ah, Captain Stevenson, follow me . . .' – all for effect, you see, and marched me brazenly to the front of the queue and said to the corporal inputting names into the computer, 'Process this officer straight away, he needs to catch a flight,' or something like that. The corporal sort of went, 'Er, OK then.' Bill kept up this pretence that I was someone important until we were out of earshot, then he said, 'Right, that's that, now we can relax.' So I avoided 'Black Adder Camp', which was a rather festering, tented camp in Al Jubail, which held all the battle casualty replacements and where the chances were you'd stay throughout the war, and miss everything.

He then stowed me away on a Hercules and we flew up country, as they say, at five hundred feet, all the way up to some grid square, unknown to anyone else, where the battalion was laagered up, and we landed on a desert airstrip in the middle of nowhere. I got out and there was nobody around. I was feeling pretty lonely and disoriented, and then I saw this column of dust over the horizon, getting closer and closer – it was like that scene in the movie *North by Northwest*. Finally this Land Rover appeared, stripped down and without the windscreen – the commanding officer, Iain Johnstone, had fought in Oman and had learned that in the desert you knocked the windscreen out so it didn't reflect the sun, so all our vehicles had no windscreens, much to the chagrin of the QM and MTO, who were all a bit upset that these Land Rovers had been trashed. But we were at war after all, and we didn't care about windscreens. In the driving seat was this Jock, as we called them in the Royal Scots, Private Jude, whom I'd known since I joined the battalion, and Colour Sergeant Jake Johnstone, whom, again, I had known since joining. Both of them had big grins on their faces. Seeing these stalwarts appear out of nowhere was really reassuring and quite a welcome sight.

It was amazing to be met in a place I'd never been before in my life, feeling pretty disorientated, and bang! there were these friendly faces coming out of nowhere. 'Jump in,' they said. So I jumped in, and governed only by their satnav, a brand-new, magic piece of kit at the time, we drove until we saw a mirage on the horizon. 'That's the battalion there, sir.' I remember getting out of the Land Rover and being surrounded by all of my friends, with their crew-cut hair, their *shemaghs* and their weapons, and I thought, Hey, I really have come home. That felt fantastic.

We really were in the middle of nowhere and we were totally self-contained, being resupplied by our own supply systems. We had our own cookhouses, kitchens, food supplies. We dug our own latrines. There were no showers or baths, of course, so you'd wash yourself in a traditional washing-up bowl, and you'd have to get the order right: you would brush your teeth first and then wash yourself or your clothes, depending on which were dirtier, and then pour this grotty water away and feel a whole lot better.

We had three weeks of fairly intensive rehearsals and manoeuvres, punctuated by training at night. Plus there was lots of admin to do, like having to get injected with the latest anthrax or bubonic plague inoculations, little things like that. We thought there was a chemical threat, so we had chemical defences:

remember this was the First Gulf War, where Saddam probably did have chemical weapons (although they never materialised).

We were very businesslike about it all. We had a strict 'no light' policy at night and all that. We wanted to ingrain a sense of rigorous military discipline into the battle group for when we knew we would need it.

We would get to a point at which we thought we were going to get the go-ahead to invade. 'You're going in tonight,' we'd be told, and then it was, 'Oh, no you're not' because we kept getting these political initiatives that some head of state had come up with as a possible last-minute solution. I think Gorbachev was the last to offer one of these.

There was no air or artillery threat, so we didn't have to live in trenches. We lived under the stars. We would sleep in our sleeping bags, looking up through the cam-nets at the night sky, and of course, in that part of the world, and that time of year, late January, February, the sky was clear, and you saw millions and millions of stars. One enduring memory was looking up late one night and seeing a triangle of three red lights threading across the sky at forty thousand feet: these were three B-52s. You'd wait a minute or two and then hold your hand to your ear, and you could hear this distant rumbling. You'd know those planes had just disgorged tonnes of conventional Second World War bombs, not much more sophisticated than that, on to the Iraqi defences, which we knew at some point we would be going in against, and you're lying there, all cozy and unthreatened in your sleeping bag, and you could imagine other people at the receiving end of this, who just happened to be born in a different place, and you had sympathy for them. But you had to steel yourself for the fact that you were going to be part of an operation that would go in and finish them off effectively, poor bastards. As a friend once said to me, 'Being born British is the first prize in the lottery of life,' and you thought to yourself, 'Yeah, I get that.'

During leisure time, I remember being out in the sunshine, writing letters home to my parents, and also to my girlfriend at the time, because you didn't have any other means of communication. There was no email, no mobile phones. In those days, we were writing aerograms – everything was about writing blueys.

I had to get the balance right between saying to my girlfriend, 'Hey this is just really exciting,' and trying to impress her, and being more cautious with letters home, knowing that my mother would be a little bit worried about it all because Saddam's pronouncement, which had been reported all over the world, was 'I'm going to turn the atmosphere into fire' or something like that. Everyone was going, 'What does that mean? Has he got nuclear weapons?' We thought this was just posturing because we knew in the end we were going to thump him. We weren't worried – well, perhaps there was a little bit of trepidation from time to time.

During the day, we would plan and have what we call 'O groups', orders groups. The O group is a carefully orchestrated presentation, led by the commanding officer and his principal staff officers, that would last several hours by the time everyone had their say. You'd get the intelligence officers to give the enemy picture. We'd have a battery commander who would talk about fire support; we'd have an engineer who'd talk about breaching obstacles and such like; and our QMs would talk about the admin side and the supplies. And of course, at this time and place, everyone was pretty focused, no one got bored or fell asleep, because every word mattered. Everyone was taking notes, and then was given time to go away and brief their own people, then come back again to rehearse a few things.

I remember taking notes on what to do to defend against a guided-missile attack on your vehicle. The tactic used then, although I don't think any of us actually tried it, was that if you were looking out of your turret, and saw a missile coming towards you, you would turn your pintle-mounted machine gun towards the missile.

Then you were given your orders. We give military orders in a certain sequence. The mission is given by the commanding officer to his subordinate level commanders, who then go away and give their extraction of orders as they become relevant to their level of command. You have a sort of cascading process, which is repetition with added value, and every time it goes down a level, you're repeating what you need to repeat from the higher commander, but adding your bit as it applies to your people.

You also get timings and what we call 'Co-ordinating Instructions', as part of that, which tell you some of the incidental details like when you're going to get fed, where the water and ammo are coming from, and what time you're refuelling. We had a squadron of tanks in our battle group and our vehicles drank a lot of diesel, so refuelling was a massive task in itself.

We respected the commanding officer for his innate feel for desert warfare. We listened to him, he was great. He was also a stickler for doing things right, for the rules of engagement, the Geneva Convention, and all that sort of stuff about how you handle prisoners of war.

I was what's called Officer Commanding Fire Support Company. Mine was not a fighting company, in that it didn't fix bayonets and charge. It was a support company, so my command comprised the mortar platoon, which basically did its own thing and worked directly to battle group headquarters; the anti-tank platoon, which tended to get split up among the companies; and the recce platoon, which, again, was doing its own thing at the front of the battle group.

But although I had pastoral care for these guys and would catch up with them as much as I could, in the conflict itself I ended up forming part of a shadow tactical HQ, by which I mean I operated with the battle group's second in command, shadowing the commanding officer's tactical headquarters. In the event that he got taken out, we would be able to move forward very quickly and take over command of the battle group. I would then be supporting the BG's second in command, who would have become the CO. So we were always only a tactical bound behind the fighting companies. That was what the CO wanted and we felt it would have worked quite well.

As far as I can remember, 23 February was the date that the ground offensive started, which was about two weeks after the air war began.

I went forward with the advance party to guide the elements of the battle group through the breach that had been carved into Saddam's defences of the border, which were mostly mines. There was a minefield lane, a gap, that we went through. It all went very smoothly, and as we didn't really know whether it would or not, that was great.

We got to what we call a forming-up position, an FUP, and moved into our attack formation for the first objective of the night. We'd been given orders to attack eight objectives that night, all of which were billed as either company-strength or battery-strength objectives.

By that stage it was getting dark. While waiting, we were told we could get out of the vehicles, although to step only in the tracks we'd already made because there was a fear of anti-personnel or anti-tank mines having been laid. We willingly got out; the vehicles were quite stuffy and it was hot of course, and we were in our NBC kit, our nuclear, biological and chemical suits – not to mention body armour and helmets. It was good to get a bit of fresh air when we could.

I remember waiting for H-Hour when we would cross the line of departure and go into the assault on the first position. It was going to be 2315 hours. All of a sudden – I nearly jumped out of my skin – there was this massive, whooshing sound that seemed to come from right behind me. I whirled round and looked, and it was the MLRS firing, the multi-launch rocket system, that was part of what we called the fire plan. This was the first time it had been used in anger. These missiles were fired out and, my word, they were impressive. You watched them arcing into the sky like huge fireworks and as they approached the target, they would burst into multiple explosive devices and rain on to the unfortunate Iraqis at the other end – another one of those 'good to be born British' moments.

The clock was ticking towards 2315, and bang on time we

advanced. The timing is everything. If you've got any sense, you set your watch by the gunner's watch, what we call 'gunner time', because they're firing the big guns. You don't want to be early because you'd drive into your own guns and if you were late you'd lose the effect because you're too far behind, so it needs to be perfectly synchronised.

One particularly vivid image is of a friend of mine, Norman Soutar, who was commanding one of the assault companies, mounting his attack. The artillery fire began and he pushed his company forward, but the timings weren't quite right and he ended up driving into his own artillery barrage. When people realised that was happening, not least him, he had a choice of either stopping and protecting himself or just pushing on through to the objective. Naturally enough, knowing him, he chose the latter and pushed on. I remember him screaming down his radio, 'Push on, push on, don't worry about all this,' meaning these airburst rounds that are pretty lethal. It was a dangerous business, albeit the threat was from your own side, but that sometimes happens. Anyway, he pushed on through. He took the objective and meanwhile the other company commander was doing similar stuff. Both of them got the Military Cross at the end of the campaign – not just for single incidents, but their general leadership under fire.

We were looking through image intensifiers. Everything was hazy green on our sights, but every now and then you'd peek out from the turret of your tank, not least to try and make sure you weren't going to get hit by one of these wire-guided anti-tank missiles. We just went through these positions one by one. There'd be sit-reps, as we call them, situation reports, coming over the radio, saying 'Yes, we've done this' and 'We've done that', but it wasn't really until it started to get light that I could have a proper look out. This time I saw two dead Iraqis, lying on the ground, shot. It was the first time I'd seen a dead body and I thought, Blimey, we've just attacked this position and killed these Iraqis. They were lying on their backs, completely flat. I can remember noticing one of their legs twisted slightly abnormally, which indicated that they weren't sleeping. I saw some gunshot wounds on them. We then saw an Iraqi crew from a T55 tank that had taken a direct hit from a Maverick missile. The crew were scattered out around this tank whose turret had been blown away, and there were three crew members, who were well dead of course. I remember thinking they looked about fourteen years old. They were very small and pretty mashed up and burned, pretty undignified, really.

In each position there was an average of about twenty Iraqis, very lightly armed. For the most part they would fire back as a token effort but very quickly give up and surrender. We developed a tactic where we flashed the headlights at them in an attempt to get them to surrender without us having to fire because we knew it was a completely unfair fight at that point. Our priority was to destroy as much Iraqi equipment as we could, but try not to kill too many Iraqis, preferably get them to surrender. As they were walking back with their hands up you'd just shout what the Arabic for food was and point back the way you'd come, and hope they would then traipse back and be picked up by the battalions who had been employed as prisoner of war handling units.

The next morning, we literally stopped in our tracks some-where in Kuwait because we had reached a natural pause. We'd achieved everything we needed to achieve and the Iraqis had retreated in relative disarray back to the road leading from Kuwait City up to Basra.

The Iraqi Army was withdrawing from Kuwait when they realised the game was up, but the conflict was still raging. Of course, there is only one route that would allow armoured formations to get out of Kuwait north quickly and that's the Basra road. They were all lined up, along this road. There were tanks. There were soft-skinned vehicles. There was a convoy of all sorts of Iraqi military vehicles snaking up this road moving at about twenty miles per hour. The Mutla Pass became infamous after an American pilot on the *World News* was heard saying, 'Hey, it's a turkey shoot out there. . .' And it was played back at a briefing in Washington, and I think George Bush suddenly thought, Shit, this is a slaughter, and it's not going to look good. It was at that point he decided enough was enough and the conflict should finish. And then, talk about 'stopped in our tracks', we got the word: President Bush has declared an end to hostilities and the war is won. We can no longer have a slaughter. We remained 'stopped in our tracks' somewhere in the middle of Kuwait. I think everyone thought that was entirely appropriate at the time, that the President had done what he intended to do, which was to remove the Iraqis from Kuwait.

The fighting on the ground had lasted a hundred hours, almost exactly, although I had by then lost track of time. I think I was beginning to suffer from a bit of sleep deprivation because we hadn't had any proper sleep at that time. You could just snatch ten minutes every now and then. After a hundred hours we'd reached the point where we thought, We've got to sleep now and we were finally told, 'OK, you can have five hours.' Well, that was a luxury. I just slept on the desert floor next to my vehicle, thinking that when I woke up, we'd be heading off again. But it very quickly became apparent that we weren't going anywhere, and that, basically, we'd won. That was it, finished, well done everyone, we've done it.

There were no great high-fives or punching of the air. For one thing, everyone was too knackered. Also, we weren't going to celebrate, partly because we lost a soldier after it all finished in a freak ammunition accident. This young soldier, who was only eighteen, had one of his rifle-launch grenades explode in his webbing. They reckoned that the movement of his vehicle had had the effect of unwinding the centrifugal fuse on the grenade, so when he took his webbing off at the end of the op, and dropped it on the ground, as you do, it detonated the grenade, which then detonated another two in the webbing and killed him instantly. That was a tragedy because we hadn't lost anyone in battle. I don't think we'd even had anyone injured, other than the chap I had replaced. So it was just cruelly ironic that this poor lad was killed, and we were slightly subdued, to put it mildly. But even without that, we didn't see this as a cause for high jinks and celebrations.

And then we all thought, Oh, now we'll go home, forgetting of course that it takes a while to get people home. We ended up having about a month out in the desert, where we established ourselves a little bit more permanently and started to do a bit of training.

We never saw the sun in the last month because Saddam had set all the oil fields ablaze and the billowing smoke obscured daylight. Even at midday we were driving with our headlights on. You could write your name in the oil on the side of every helicopter that came in because it had flown through this oily atmosphere.

Eventually, we started the trip home, flying directly to Al Jubail from a grid reference somewhere in the Kuwaiti desert. They carved out an airstrip for a Hercules to land and we all got loaded operationally on to this Herc – in other words, all the seats had been taken out and everyone sat cross-legged on the floor, about eighty people, all cheek by jowl. The Herc pilot asked over the intercom, 'Who wants to see the burning oil fires? We can fly over the Kuwaiti oil fields on our way down to Al Jubail.'

Everyone said, 'Yeah, that'll be good.'

'OK,' he said. 'I'll open the back door of the Herc so you can all see out when I fly over.'

And that's what he did. He flew very low and opened the back door. None of us had safety belts – we were just sitting on the floor of the aircraft. There were these burning oil fields and everyone exclaimed – but then suddenly the aircraft lurched violently because of the thermals the fires had created and I watched the whole of my company rise almost two feet off the floor like levitating Tibetan monks and bounce back down again. Everything then went a bit quiet up in the cockpit and the pilot rapidly shut the back door. The Herc climbed quite high out of the way and we didn't hear much from him after that. I think he realised that hadn't been a very clever thing to do.

At Al Jubail we were reunited with our vehicles. I got into my Warrior and we drove through Kuwait, not in triumph, but people who saw us regarded us as victors. We were heads up in our turrets at this stage, driving along main roads, and being met with spontaneous applause and cheering, and all that. It felt extraordinary, actually. You did feel like liberators.

We flew back to the UK on a British Airways jumbo jet. It's the only time I've ever been in first class. The officers were all put in first class, the sergeants' mess were put in business class and all the poor old other ranks were chucked in economy.

I think if I'd had a wife and children to come back to, arriving home would have been a very emotional moment, but because I was single in those days, it was like, 'Right, let's get back to camp quickly, get changed, and go out to a bar somewhere.' But it was an exciting time, which had put us on the front page of every newspaper in the world for the previous few weeks. We all felt that we'd done a great job, we'd succeeded in what we'd set out to do, and had a really exciting time.

Subsequently, of course, there was a lot of debate about whether we should have gone on into Baghdad, and all that, but it was very clear to us at the time that the United Nation's Resolution allowed us to kick the Iraqis out of Kuwait, but there was no mandate to do any more. Nor did we think it was a good idea because we knew if we kicked Saddam out of Baghdad, what would we have done then? Although of course that scenario was played out again a decade or so later.

LANCE SERGEANT DAMIAN THOMAS
'We think it's funny as hell . . .'

If 'I love the Army, the Army's for me' is one extreme end of the scale and 'This is absolute shit, I don't want to do this any more' is the other, I am somewhere in the middle. I love being in the Army, but I would rather stay out of Afghanistan.

I have done three tours away from home, six months for each tour, and all I could think about each time was going home. Living in an FOB is hard. I don't like being in the middle of nowhere. You are covered in dust, thousands of miles away from home, and all you have got to eat is Super Noodles. Flies are constantly around your face. They drive you mad. You are never clean because the sand is always sticking to your sweat, and the heat makes you very tired, very quickly. You never get used to it.

You soon think, I want to go back home to GB. I want to see roads. I want to get into my car and drive it for miles, instead of walking everywhere for miles. I want to hear a female voice. I want to see girls in short skirts. I want to go into a building with air conditioning or be able to order a pizza. All these things make you wonder why you have left them to come out here. The only thing that drove me was money. You get paid an extra £13 a day while you are on tour, and because you're in a dustbowl thousands of miles from the nearest shops, there's nothing to buy, so you come back with a lot of extra money, which is important right now because I have got a family to look after. Also, I would love another kid. So everything I do is money-orientated.

On this last tour – which I've just come back from – we spent two months in Garmsir. Our main mission was to probe and dominate no man's land, defend what ground we had taken in the first place and then dominate the surrounding area. When we first got there it was quite barren, but as the summer came on, things just grew, like really pink tropical flowers that bloomed out of the dust, which were quite nice. Also, Garmsir is a plain surrounded by mountains, and this massive river is flowing next to you, which we jumped into now and then to get a soak – that was morale all round.

We were doing ops near enough every single night until we got relieved in place by the Woofers.* From there we were told we were going to get a buckshee time for a month and moved on up to Sangin, which was a lot easier than Garmsir.

From Sangin we went to Gereshk, which was a hard time for the whole company. FOB Arnhem was the worst place we stayed. It was built in the desert, so it was miles away from anywhere. I could understand why they did this. They wanted to be able to see if the enemy approached, but it was living like a hobo. It was built out of Hesco, so you had to build a shelter under

*Worcestershire and Sherwood Foresters Regiment.

your poncho, which magnifies the heat, and the Hesco doesn't let any air in, so you just lived under a poncho in a dustbowl in sixty-degree heat. Inside there was nothing. No luxuries came. We didn't have a TV. We didn't have electric. We just woke up in the morning, sweated and went out on patrol, and if you didn't do that, you just sat there and melted.

Seeing someone killed can change you. Some people on that tour saw someone get shot or killed and crumbled in on themselves. They just couldn't cope and had to be sent back home. I knew all these lads who were killed, all of them. I felt sorry for their relatives, but I didn't cry. I don't know why. Maybe it's a typical man hiding his emotions. So I knew I could cope with all that, and I could crack on and do the job I came here to do. It hasn't changed me, but it has made me appreciate things a lot more. I was thinking it could quite easily have been me.

There're going to be times when everybody feels low. For instance, I had to carry a friend on my shoulders for a kilometre. He was already dead. He had no armour and when I was finished, I was covered in his blood, and I thought, I don't know how I am going to carry on doing this job.

But you put on a piece of music and people start dancing; people make volleyball courts and play games like bare-arse football, where you stand against the wall with your bare arse hanging out and people have got to kick a ball at your arse as hard as they can – which we think is funny as hell and it keeps our mind off the things we're doing.

We had some good laughs at Arnhem. We played football most nights. Then someone got some boxing gloves sent to them in parcels and we started boxing matches: Marines vs the

Grenadiers, then between the snipers and the anti-tanks, and then 1 Platoon played 2 Platoon, and then section officers got involved. It was something to break up the time, something different – rather than doing the same thing every single day, which was get up, go on patrol and sweat.

The Taliban are hard to find, although I don't understand why. We're the ones that wear camouflage, while they wear a white dish-dash. Also, they have no tactics – they fire a couple of shots and run. Obviously, they are not that great at fighting – that's why we have lost 250-plus since 2001, but we have killed hundreds and hundreds of them. Often it's just luck when they kill one of us. Take the first guy from the battalion who got shot, Guardsman Davison. He was manning a machine gun after ten days of being in Garmsir. Shots went everywhere and they got him in the face. You couldn't have done that shot if you had tried and tried, but unfortunately they got lucky and he got killed.

We had a detachment of Engineers arrive. They brought in generators, so we got electric in the buildings and could plug things in, which meant we could see what we were doing, instead of using torchlight. They dug a well, so we had constant water then, although it was chlorinated, so it tasted like swimming-pool water – drink that for six months and it sends you mad.

The company sergeant major put in the request for luxuries – basically, every time there's a supply run, we can order things we want or need. You think of anything that will make your life a little bit easier and the Army does their best to provide it. You don't always get what you ask for, but if you don't ask you don't get.

They sent board games down, so we had a crack at Monopoly

and played that together. We said we wanted a TV, so they sent us this crappy old twenty-eight-inch 1970s one, but at the end of the day, it was a TV – and on top of that they sent a satellite. We had connection to the British Forces Broadcasting Service, so we could still keep watching *EastEnders*. That was on the ball; it felt like we were getting some home comforts.

We were quite happy out there. In the Guards we have got quite a respect for the rank system, everything is 'Yes sir, no sir, three bags full sir.' However, working so intensely out in the middle of nowhere closes the rank system, and by the end of the tour it was more like a 'Yes mate, no mate' kind of thing. It was hard to break that familiarity when we got back.

Our commanding officer was Lieutenant Colonel Carew Hatherley, who got a Queen's Commendation for Valuable Service. He's one of the best commanding officers I have ever worked for. He knows what he's talking about and isn't afraid to make decisions. And somehow he just had this knack of giving orders in such a way that you wanted to do them. Plus, I wouldn't be surprised if he knew 80 per cent of everyone's names, so every time he saw you, he knew who he was talking to. Also, he always had a smile on his face and that's what you need from a bloke who wants something doing, you don't want a CO who is going around shouting at you all the time – that's the sergeant major's job.

But actually the sergeant major was brilliant as well, because he wasn't into micro-management. He only intervened if he needed to, so we were able to get on with our jobs without looking over our shoulders.

You are supposed to get two weeks' rest and recuperation in

the middle of your tour, but it doesn't always fall in the middle because you can't have everyone going at the same time. I went on leave after four and a half months in theatre, home to Leicester.

So one day I'm in a FOB in the desert, the next I'm dropped off at Bastion and on a plane to the UK. My wife met me at the airport. I came out still wearing body armour and quite mucky, plus I had long hair that she had never seen me with, and a beard, which she also had never seen. I was so skinny, I just looked like skin and bones, and she went, 'Oh my God,' and burst into tears, which I expected her to do anyway.

We got into the car and I had the biggest, fattest McDonald's on the way home and then she made me a Sunday roast, and I had a bottle of wine. We had a little chat and she told me what had been going on and I told her my stuff – you only get twenty minutes' phone call every week, so I had just told her snippets, although at the end of the day, I don't really tell her much about work anyway. First of all because she's never really asked, but also, I don't want to scare her. Why would I want to tell her, 'Oh, one of my mates got blown up, and I carried him for a K, and when I put him down in the back of a wagon I was covered in his blood, and the next time I saw his face was in the paper stating he was dead.' Her heart would jump down her throat and she would think, Oh my God, he's got to go there again in two years' time, so then she is going to say, 'I don't want you to go.'

But it was a good R & R. I like my bed. I like getting up any time I want and not having to worry about being woken up in the middle of the night with the sound of gunfire or somebody shouting, 'Stand to.' I just wanted to do normal things, nothing spectacular. I don't want to visit Paris or anything like that. I like being with my wife and going shopping, and I went camping with the wife and the little girl too.

On the last day I woke up at 5 a.m., made the wife a cup of tea, she drove me to the airport and I had a last cigarette with her as we said our goodbyes. Then I sent her off because she'd started crying again.

Everyone knows when you have been on leave because you are the only one who has had a shave and a haircut, and all the lads are back to being gorillas again. You sit down and straight away people will tell you what's been going on while you've been away. It's strange. You tell them what you did in the UK, but you want to hear much more about what's going on in Afghanistan. You want to know if anyone has got into a firefight and has anyone been hurt?

That last month was probably the steadiest month. We were winding down the tour, looking towards the handover to the Coldstream Guards. The ops started to slow down: instead of every night, they were every other night, and then they went on to every three nights. People started to shave again and try to get back into the mindset of discipline.

Then the Coldstream Guards arrived and set up sleeping bags in the middle of the car park area we had made, which was just a dustbowl. They came round at night time while we were doing our usual stuff, like playing cards and Monopoly. They said, 'Hi lads, how's it been?' and we told them the major bad points, which is is that people get hurt, especially if this is their first tour. I said, 'Don't pay lip service to anything. Don't be complacent. When you are patrolling, make sure you are looking around because when it comes it's a surprise. You never can be ready for everything. You've just got to be able to react when it happens.'

Then we wished them luck and that was that. The chopper picked us up the following morning and they moved into where we had been.

ABBREVIATIONS/GLOSSARY

AK47	assault rifle used by the Soviet Army in the Second World War and still widely in use
ANA	Afghan National Army
ATM	anti-tank missile
ATO	ammunition technical officer
ATR	Army Training Regiment
BC	battery commander
bergen	heavy-duty canvas rucksack used by the Army
BG	Battle Group
bluey	free aerogram letter available for troops in combat
BQMS	battery quartermaster sergeant
CASEVAC	casualty evacuation
Challenger 2	British Army's main battle tank
CO	commanding officer
COB	contingency operating base
DFID	Department for International Development
EOD	explosive ordnance disposal
FOB	forward operating base

FSG	fire support group
GPMG	general purpose machine gun
GPS	global positioning system
Green Zone	in Afghanistan the three-hundred-kilometre strip of farmland downstream from the Kajaki dam and through the Upper Gereshk Valley. In Iraq the heavily fortified ten-square-kilometre zone in the centre of Baghdad that served as the headquarters of the city's international presence.
Herrick	codename under which British operations in the war in Afghanistan have been conducted
Hesco	prefabricated, multi-cellular defence system made of steel mesh lined with synthetic resin
HLS	helicopter landing site
IDF	indirect fire
IED	improvised explosive device
IRT	immediate response team
ISAF	International Security Assistance Force (in Afghanistan)
ISO	shipping container used as stores, including arms and ammunition, or as temporary offices, living quarters and operating theatres
ISTAR	intelligence, surveillance, target acquisition and reconnaissance
JOC	joint operational command
JTAC	joint tactical air controller
laager	(as in 'laager up') defensive position
LEC	local employed civilian
LMG	light machine gun

Mastiff	heavily armoured patrol vehicle
MERT	medical emergency response team
MIA	missing in action
MTO	motor transport officer
Naafi	Navy, Army and Air Force Institutes, HM Forces' official trading organisation
NGO	non-governmental organisation
OC	officer commanding
OMLT	operational mentoring liaison team
OP	observation post
OTC	Officer Training Corps
PJHQ	permanent joint headquarters
PTSD	post-traumatic stress disorder
QM	quartermaster
QRF	quick reaction force
RAMC	Royal Army Medical Corps
R & R	rest and recuperation
rank slide	flat cloth sleeve bearing rank worn on the shoulder strap of uniform
REME	Royal Electrical and Mechanical Engineers
RLC	Royal Logistic Corps
ROE	rules of engagement
RPG	rocket-propelled grenade
RSM	regimental sergeant major
sangar	protected observation point
Scimitar	fast armoured reconnaissance tracked vehicle. Top speed 80kph
SLR	self-loading rifle
Snatch	armoured Land Rover

Telic   codename under which British operations in Iraq
             were conducted between 2003 and 2009
TIC   troops in contact
2iC   second in command
UAV   unmanned aerial vehicle
UNAMIR   United Nations Assistance Mission for Rwanda
Viking   armoured all-terrain vehicle
Warrior   heavily armoured infantry fighting vehicle
WMIK   weapon mount installation kit

ABOUT THE AUTHOR

Danny Danziger has written eleven books on a range of diverse subjects, including *The Year 1000*, which went to number one and stayed on the bestseller list for seven months. Danny has a weekly interview column in the *Sunday Times*, 'Best of Times, Worst of Times', which over twelve years has won many accolades and awards.